Evidence-Based
Instruction in Reading

Phonemic Awareness

Evidence-Based Instruction in Reading

A Professional Development Guide to Phonemic Awareness

Maryann Mraz

University of North Carolina at Charlotte

Nancy D. Padak

Kent State University

Timothy V. Rasinski

Kent State University

PEARSON

Boston • New York • San Francisco
Mexico City • Montreal • Toronto • London • Madrid • Munich • Paris
Hong Kong • Singapore • Tokyo • Cape Town • Sydney

Executive Editor: *Aurora Martínez Ramos*
Series Editorial Assistant: *Lynda Giles*
Marketing Manager: *Danae April*
Production Editor: *Gregory Erb*
Editorial Production Service: *Publishers' Design and Production Services, Inc.*
Composition Buyer: *Linda Cox*
Manufacturing Buyer: *Linda Morris*
Electronic Composition: *Publishers' Design and Production Services, Inc.*
Photo Researcher: *Annie Pickert*
Cover Designer: *Kristina Mose-Libon*

For related titles and support materials, visit our online catalog at www.ablongman.com.

Between the time website information is gathered and then published, it is not unusual for some sites to have closed. Also, the transcription of URLs can result in typographical errors. The publisher would appreciate notification where these errors occur so that they may be corrected in subsequent editions.

Cataloging-in-Publication data unavailable at press time.

ISBN-10: 0-205-45628-6
ISBN-13: 978-0-205-45628-4

Printed in the United States of America

10 9 8 7 6 5 4 3 2 1   RRD-VA   11 10 09 08 07

Photo Credits: Page 1: © Lindfors Photography; pp. 13, 49, 63: © IndexOpen; p. 33: © Image 100.

Among us, we have been teachers and teacher educators for nearly 100 years! During this time, we have developed deep and abiding respect for teachers and trust in their ability to offer their students the very best possible instruction. Yet we also agree with librarian John Cotton Dana (1856–1929), who said, "Who dares to teach must never cease to learn."

Our careers have been marked by continual learning. We dedicate this book to all who have taught us and all whom we have taught—all who have dared to teach.

NP
TR
MM
EN
BZ

Contents

SERIES INTRODUCTION: EVIDENCE-BASED INSTRUCTION IN READING:
A PROFESSIONAL DEVELOPMENT GUIDE   xi

    The National Reading Panel Report   xii

    Professional Development in Literacy   xv

    Using the Books   xv

    Overview of Book Content   xvi

INTRODUCTION: PHONEMIC AWARENESS   xix

CHAPTER 1

Phonemic Awareness: What Does Research Tell Us?   1

    What Is Phonemic Awareness?   2

    Why Is Phonemic Awareness Important?   3

    How Can I Help Students Acquire Phonemic Awareness?   5

    Professional Development Suggestions   10

CHAPTER 2

Instructional Strategies for Phonemic Awareness Development   13

    Guiding Principles for Instruction   14

    Professional Development Suggestions   16

    Strategy Suggestions   18

    Phonemic Awareness Materials and Programs   31

    Professional Development Suggestions   32

CHAPTER 3

Assessing Phonemic Awareness Development   *33*

Big Ideas   34

Evaluate Your Current Assessment Practices   37

Ideas for Assessment   39

Plans for Change   42

Professional Development Suggestions   43

Reflection Protocol   45

CHAPTER 4

Fostering Home–School Connections   *49*

Supporting Phonemic Awareness at Home   50

Engaging Families in Home Literacy Activities   52

Literacy Tips for Children Ages 0–3 Years Old   52

Literacy Tips for Children Ages 4–6 Years Old   54

Literacy Tips for Children Ages 7–8 years Old   55

Communicating with Families   57

Professional Development Suggestions   61

CHAPTER 5

Resources   *63*

Common Rimes (Phonograms or Word Families)   64

Letter Sounds in Action   66

Children's Books for Phonemic Awareness Development   66

Alphabet Books   69

Songs for Phonemic Awareness Development   69

Web Resources for Phonemic Awareness Development   70

Professional Resources for Teachers   72

Goal Planning   74

Book Club

APPENDIX **A**

Book Club Ideas   77

APPENDIX B

Notes   81

REFERENCES   93

Series Introduction

Evidence-Based Instruction in Reading: A Professional Development Guide

Better than a thousand days of diligent study is one day spent with a great teacher.

JAPANESE PROVERB

*L*earning to read is perhaps a young child's greatest school accomplishment. Of course, reading is the foundation for success in all other school subjects. Reading is critical to a person's own intellectual development, later economic success, and the pleasure that is to be found in life.

Similarly, teaching a child to read is one of the greatest accomplishments a teacher can ever hope for. And yet, reading and teaching reading are incredibly complex activities. The reading process involves elements of a person's psychological, physical, linguistic, cognitive, emotional, and social world. Teaching reading, of course, involves all these and more. Teachers must orchestrate the individuality of each child they encounter; the physical layout of the classroom and attendant materials; their own colleagues, parents, and school administration; the school's specified curriculum; and their own style of teaching! The popular cliché that "reading is not rocket science" perhaps underestimates the enormity of the task of teaching children to read.

The complexity of teaching reading can be, quite simply, overwhelming. How does a teacher teach and find mastery of the various skills in reading, attending to the school and state curricular guidelines, using an appropriate variety of materials, while simultaneously meeting the individual needs of all children in the classroom? We

xii

································

SERIES
INTRODUCTION

*Evidenced-Based
Instruction in
Reading*

think that it was because of the enormous complexity of this task that many teachers resorted to prepackaged reading programs to provide the structure and sequence for a given grade level. Basal reading programs, for example, provide some assurance that at least some of the key skills and content for reading are covered within a given period of time.

The problem with prepackaged programs is that they are not sensitive to the culture of the classroom, school, and community, the individual children in the classroom, and the instructional style of the teacher. The one-size-fits-all approach adopted by such programs—with, of course, the best of intentions—resulted in programs that met the minimal needs of the students, that lacked the creative flair that only a teacher can give a program, and that absolved teachers of a good deal of the accountability for teaching their students. If children failed to learn to read, it was the fault of the program.

The fact of the matter is that many children failed to learn to read up to expectations using prepackaged programs. The results of periodic assessments of U.S. students' reading achievement, most notably the National Assessment of Educational Progress, have demonstrated little, if any, growth in student reading achievement over the past 30 years. This lack of growth in literacy achievement is at least partially responsible for equally dismal results in student growth in other subject areas that depend highly on a student's ability to read.

The National Reading Panel Report

Having noticed this disturbing trend, the National Reading Panel (NRP) was formed by the United States Congress in 1996 and given the mandate of reviewing the scientific research related to reading and determining those areas that science has shown have the greatest promise for improving reading achievement in the elementary grades. In 2000, the NRP came out with its findings. Essentially, the panel found that the existing scientific research points to five particular areas of reading that have the greatest promise of increasing reading achievement: phonemic awareness, phonics and word decoding, reading fluency, vocabulary, and reading comprehension. Additionally, the NRP indicated that investments in teachers, through professional development activities, hold promise of improving student reading achievement.

xiii

SERIES
INTRODUCTION
*Evidenced-Based
Instruction in
Reading*

The findings of the NRP have been the source of considerable controversy, yet they have been used by the federal and state governments, as well as local school systems, to define and mandate reading instruction. In particular, the federal Reading First program has mandated that any school receiving funds from Reading First must embed within its reading curriculum direct and systematic teaching of phonemic awareness, phonics, reading fluency, vocabulary, and comprehension. The intent of the mandate, of course, is to provide students with the instruction that is based on best evidence that it will have a positive impact on students' reading achievement.

Although we may argue about certain aspects of the findings of the National Reading Panel, in particular what it left out of its report of effective instructional principles, we find ourselves in solid agreement with the panel that the five elements that it identified are indeed critical to success in learning to read.

Phonemic awareness is crucial to early reading development. Students must develop an ability to think about the sounds of language and to manipulate those sounds in various ways—to blend sounds, to segment words into sounds, and so on. An inability to deal with language sounds in this way will set the stage for difficulty in phonics and word decoding. To sound out a word, which is essentially what phonics requires of students, readers must have adequate phonemic awareness. Yet, some estimates indicate that as many as 20 percent of young children in the United States do not have sufficient phonemic awareness to profit fully from phonics instruction.

Phonics, or the ability to decode written words in text, is clearly essential for reading. Students who are unable to accurately decode at least 90 percent of the words they encounter while reading will have difficulty gaining appropriate meaning from what they read. We prefer to expand the notion of phonics to word decoding. Phonics, or using the sound–symbol relationship between letters and words, is, without doubt, an important way to solve unknown words. However, there are other methods to decode written words. These include attending to the prefixes, suffixes, and base elements of longer words; examining words for rimes (word families) and other letter patterns; using meaningful context to determine unknown words; dividing longer words into smaller parts through syllabication; and making words part of one's sight vocabulary, words recognized instantly and by sight. Good readers are able to employ all of these strategies and more. Appropriately, instruction needs to be aimed at helping students develop proficiency in learning to decode words using multiple strategies.

Reading fluency refers to the ability to read words quickly, as well as accurately, and with appropriate phrasing and expression. Fluent readers are able to decode words so effortlessly that they can direct their cognitive resources away from the low-level decoding task and to the more important meaning-making or comprehension part of reading. For a long time, fluency was a relatively neglected area of the reading curriculum. In recent years, however, educators have come to realize that although fluency deals with the ability to efficiently and effortlessly decode words, it is critical to good reading comprehension and needs to be part of any effective reading curriculum.

Word and concept meaning is the realm of *vocabulary.* Not only must readers be able to decode or sound out words but they must also know what these words mean. Instruction aimed at expanding students' repertoire of word meanings and deepening their understanding of already known words is essential to reading success. Thus, vocabulary instruction is an integral part of an effective instructional program in reading.

Accurate and fluent decoding of words, coupled with knowledge of word meanings, may seem to ensure *comprehension.* However, there is more to it than that. Good readers also actively engage in constructing meaning, beyond individual words, from what they read. That is, they engage in meaning-constructing strategies while they read. These include ensuring that readers employ their background knowledge for the topics they encounter in reading. It also means that they ask questions, make predictions, and create mental images while they read. Additionally, readers monitor their reading comprehension and know when to stop and check things out when things begin to go awry—that is, when readers become aware that they are not making adequate sense out of what they are reading. These are just some of the comprehension strategies and processes good readers use while they read to ensure that they understand written texts. These same strategies must be introduced and taught to students in an effective reading instruction program.

Phonemic awareness, phonics/decoding, reading fluency, vocabulary, and comprehension are the five essential elements of effective reading programs identified by the National Reading Panel. We strongly agree with the findings of the NRP—these elements must be taught to students in their reading program.

Rather than get into in-depth detail on research and theory related to these topics, our intent in this series is to provide you with a collection of simple, practical, and relatively easy-to-implement instructional strategies, proven through research and actual practice, for teaching each of the five essential components. We think you will find the books in this series readable and practical. Our hope is that you will use these books as a set of handbooks for developing more effective and engaging reading instruction for all your students.

XV
....

SERIES
INTRODUCTION
*Evidenced-Based
Instruction in
Reading*

Professional Development in Literacy

Effective literacy instruction requires teachers to be knowledgeable, informed professionals capable of assessing student needs and responding to those needs with an assortment of instructional strategies. Whether you are new to the field or a classroom veteran, ongoing professional development is imperative. Professional development influences instructional practices which, in turn, affect student achievement (Wenglinsky, 2000). Effective professional development is not simply an isolated program or activity; rather, it is an ongoing, consistent learning effort where links between theoretical knowledge and the application of that knowledge to daily classroom practices are forged in consistent and meaningful ways (Renyi, 1998).

Researchers have noted several characteristics of effective professional development: It must be grounded in research-based practices; it must be collaborative, allowing teachers ample opportunities to share knowledge, as well as teaching and learning challenges, among colleagues; and it must actively engage teachers in assessing, observing, and responding to the learning and development of their students (Darling-Hammond & McLaughlin, 1995). This professional development series, *Evidence-Based Instruction in Reading: A Professional Development Guide* is intended to provide a roadmap for systematic, participatory professional development initiatives.

Using the Books

The *Evidence-Based Instruction in Reading* series consists of five professional development books, each addressing one major component of literacy instruction identified by the National Reading Panel and widely accepted in the field as necessary for effective literacy programs: phonemic awareness, phonics, vocabulary, fluency, and comprehension. These five components are not, by any means, the only components needed for effective literacy instruction. Access to appropriate reading materials, productive home–school connections, and a desire to learn to read and write are also critical pieces of the

xvi

SERIES
INTRODUCTION

*Evidenced-Based
Instruction in
Reading*

literacy puzzle. It is our hope, however, that by focusing in depth on each of the five major literacy components, we can provide educators and professional development facilitators with concrete guidelines and suggestions for enhancing literacy instruction. Our hope is that teachers who read, reflect, and act on the information in these books will be more able to provide effective instruction in each of the five essential areas of reading.

Each book is intended to be used by professional development facilitators, be they administrators, literacy coaches, reading specialists, and/or classroom teachers, and program participants as they engage in professional development initiatives or in-service programs within schools or school districts. The use of the series can be adapted to meet the specific needs and goals of a group of educators. For example, a school may choose to hold a series of professional development sessions on each of the five major components of literacy instruction; it may choose to focus in depth on one or two components that are most relevant to its literacy program; or it may choose to focus on specific aspects, such as assessment or instructional strategies, of one or more of the five areas.

The books may also be useful in professional book club settings. An icon, included at spots for book club discussion, mark times when you might wish to share decisions about your own classroom to get colleagues' feedback. You might also want to discuss issues or solve problems with colleagues. Appendix A lists several other possible book club activities. These are listed by chapter and offer opportunities to delve into issues mentioned in the chapters in greater depth. It is important that, in collaboration with teachers, professional development needs be carefully assessed so that the appropriate content can be selected to meet those needs.

Overview of Book Content

To begin each book in the series, Chapter 1 presents a literature review that defines the literacy component to be addressed in that book, explains why this component is important in the context of a complete and balanced literacy program, and synthesizes key research findings that underlie the recommendations for evidence-based instructional practices that follow in subsequent chapters. The conclusion of Chapter 1 invites professional development program participants to analyze, clarify, extend, and discuss the material presented in this chapter.

Chapter 2 outlines general principles for instruction. Participants are asked to evaluate their own instructional practices and to plan for refinement of those practices based on their students' needs. Each suggested instructional strategy in this chapter is based on the research presented in Chapter 1 and includes the purpose, necessary materials, and procedures for implementation. Ideas for engaging professional development participants in extended discussions related to phonemic awareness, phonics, vocabulary, fluency, or comprehension are offered at the end of Chapter 2.

Chapter 3 begins by presenting broad themes for effective assessment such as focusing on critical information, looking for patterns of behavior, recognizing developmental progressions, deciding how much assessment information is needed, using instructional situations for assessment purposes, using assessment information to guide instruction, and sharing assessment information with children and families. At the end of Chapter 3, professional development participants are asked to evaluate their current assessment practices, draw conclusions about needed change, and develop plans for change. The conclusion of the chapter provides vignettes and questions designed to generate collaborative discussion about and concrete ways to enhance connections between assessment and classroom instruction.

Chapter 4 invites participants to think beyond classroom-based strategies by examining activities that can be recommended to families to support children's development of phonemic awareness, phonics, vocabulary, fluency, and comprehension at home. The final chapter provides a variety of print- and Web-based resources to support instruction in phonemic awareness, phonics, vocabulary, fluency, or comprehension.

Together, the information and activities included in these books, whether used as is or selectively, will foster careful consideration of research-based practice. Professional development participants will learn about the research that supports their current practices and will be guided to identify areas for improvement in their classroom programs.

The need for new programs and methods for teaching reading is questionable. What is without question is the need for great teachers of reading—teachers who are effective, inspiring, and knowledgeable of children and reading. This series of books is our attempt to guide teachers into a deeper understanding of their craft and art—to help already good teachers become the great teachers that we need.

Introduction

Phonemic Awareness

*T*hink back to your own early literacy school experiences. How did you learn to read? What kinds of instructional activities do you recall from your elementary classrooms? Which experiences made learning to read enjoyable? Were there any that you found to be difficult or mundane?

Typically, teachers have difficulty recalling phonemic awareness activities that were part of their own school routines. Indeed, until the past decade or so, the importance of phonemic awareness as part of the needed foundation for early literacy instruction was not widely recognized. Traditionally, prekindergarten and early elementary classrooms emphasized phonics instruction. So, perhaps you recall classrooms where the analytic or whole-to-part approach to reading was the norm: Students were first taught a series of sight words and then taught the phonics rules or generalizations that were relevant to those sight words. They were expected to apply those generalizations to other new words they encountered. Workbooks and practice exercises were hallmarks of this approach to phonics instruction (Harris & Hodges, 1995). Or maybe you recall early reading instruction that used a synthetic or part-to-whole approach to phonics. Students were taught letter names and letter sounds. They were drilled on those isolated sound–letter connections before blending separate sounds to create words (Vacca et al., 2006).

Current research, however, has shown the importance of placing some instructional emphasis on children's developing ability to listen to, produce, and manipulate the sounds of oral language separate from the letter names that are used to represent those sounds. Phonemic awareness, the ability to focus on and manipulate the spoken sounds of language, is now widely recognized as one essential element of effective early literacy instruction.

Before delving into the material that follows about research on phonemic awareness, instructional strategies, assessment, and resources, we recommend that you examine your current understanding, beliefs, and possible misconceptions about phonemic awareness. The following multiple-choice questions can serve as a starting point to activate background knowledge on this topic:

1. _____ Phonemic awareness is

    a. a necessary condition for success in phonics
    b. essentially the same as phonics
    c. a result of good phonics instruction

2. _____ Which of the following is a good way to teach phonemic awareness?

    a. play with rhymes and poetry
    b. teach the alphabet
    c. teach sound–symbol relationships
    d. all of the above

3. _____ Besides phonemic awareness, which of the following are good predictors of early reading success?

    a. conventions of print/concepts of print
    b. alphabet knowledge/letter-name knowledge
    c. visual acuity and tracking ability
    d. A and B above
    e. none of the above

4. _____ "Invented spelling"

    a. involves a child's attempt to make sense of the sound–symbol system
    b. should normally be considered undesirable and corrected
    c. helps to build children's phonemic awareness and phonics knowledge
    d. A and C above
    e. none of the above

5. _____ The smallest unit of sound in language is a

    a. morpheme
    b. grapheme
    c. phoneme
    d. letter

6. _____ According to research, which is the best predictor of reading success?

    a. IQ
    b. SES status
    c. phonemic awareness
    d. birth order

7. _____ Children's approximations can be used to

    a. teach other children phonetic generalizations
    b. assess developmental progress in reading only
    c. assess developmental progress in reading and writing

(The answer key is at the end of this section.)

    Whether you struggled with some of these questions or answered them all correctly, it is our hope that the chapters that follow in this professional development tool will clarify and enhance your knowledge of phonemic awareness, the role that it plays in early literacy instruction, and how to teach and assess your students' phonemic awareness ability as they develop as readers and writers.

    As you prepare to begin this professional development program, we invite you to consider and discuss with colleagues the following items that may help frame your interpretation and application of the material in this book. Take some time now to write notes about these aspects of your literacy program, particularly with regard to the phonemic awareness aspect:

- Describe the conditions under which you work.

    _____
    _____
    _____

- Describe the major goals of your program.

    _____
    _____
    _____

- What are the principles that ground, or serve as a rationale for, your program?

    _____
    _____
    _____

- Describe your daily schedule or classroom routine, particularly as it relates to literacy instruction.

  _____

  _____

  _____

- Describe the materials that you currently use for literacy instruction.

  _____

  _____

  _____

- How are parents involved in your literacy program?

  _____

  _____

  _____

- How do you currently assess student progress?

  _____

  _____

  _____

The chapters that follow are intended to provide an organizational framework for phonemic awareness instruction that will assist you in identifying elements that are effective and offering suggestions when modifications need to be made. Chapter 1 presents an overview of current research and professional literature on phonemic awareness. Research-based answers are provided for questions such as why phonemic awareness instruction is important, how phonemic awareness instruction can be used most effectively, who benefits from phonemic awareness instruction, and in which order phonemic awareness skills are best learned. The end of the chapter invites you to analyze, clarify, extend, discuss, and apply information learned from this chapter.

Chapter 2 focuses on research-based instructional practices. General principles for early literacy instruction are presented first. Then, you are asked to use a semantic feature analysis to evaluate your own instructional practices, considering both instructional practices that are effective and those that are in need of fine-tuning. The strategy suggestions that follow include instructional ideas for sound activities that mirror the developmental stages of phonemic awareness, listening, rhyming and alliteration games, sound boxes, and ways to make concrete connections between sounds and letters.

Chapter 3 focuses on assessment and begins by describing broad truisms of assessment that can be applied to all aspects of literacy learning. After working with these broad assessment ideas, you are asked to examine more closely your own current assessment practices in terms of both critical elements of phonemic awareness and how you assess individual students. Vignettes and questions at the end of the chapter offer opportunities for collaboration on how to address phonemic awareness issues. Graphic organizers are provided for goal planning, reflection, and curriculum alignment.

Chapter 4 moves beyond classroom-based strategies and considers recommendations for families to use at home to support their children's phonemic awareness development. Parents' frequently asked questions about phonemic awareness are also addressed in this chapter.

Chapter 5 provides resources for teaching phonemic awareness, including examples of common rimes and suggestions for action phonics. Also included are examples of children's literature that are particularly helpful for phonemic awareness instruction, and examples of both alphabet books and songs for developing phonemic awareness. Professional resources, including Web resources and professional literature for teachers, round out this final chapter.

Throughout the book you will find ample room to make notes about various aspects of planning and implementing effective phonemic awareness instruction. We encourage you to use these spaces to record insights and ideas that are particularly pertinent to your own instruction. Doing so should provide you with the kind of concrete plan of action you'll need to offer students more consistent and effective opportunities to develop their phonemic awareness.

Answer Key: 1–a; 2–a; 3–d; 4–c; 5–c; 6–b; 7–c

Evidence-Based Instruction in Reading

Phonemic Awareness

Phonemic Awareness: What Does Research Tell Us?

*W*alk into Mrs. Chapman's kindergarten classroom and you'll see an environment brimming with opportunities for language play. Song lyrics, poetry, jump-rope chants, simple riddles, and nursery rhymes all provide enjoyable and engaging opportunities for children to hear and use the sounds of language. Knowledgeable teachers can use early literacy experiences, such as these, to help nurture children's enthusiasm for language and to establish a foundation for further reading and writing development.

The topic of early reading instruction has, in recent years, generated much discussion among educators, researchers, and policymakers (Calfee & Norman, 2000). Policy initiatives at both the state and federal levels support evidence-based programs that assess and instruct students at the earliest stages of literacy development. Although a range of opinions has existed about some early literacy issues, there is widespread agreement that research supports the inclusion of phonemic awareness instruction in early literacy programs. *The Report of the National Reading Panel* (National Reading Panel, 2000) identified phonemic awareness as an essential element for young children's reading success. The panel found that phonemic awareness instruction helps build a foundation for future understanding of the alphabet system and of the connection of that system to meaningful reading and writing. Teaching children to manipulate the sounds used in language helps them learn to read.

Phonemic awareness instruction is, of course, one piece of the complete literacy instruction puzzle. It is not a quick fix for struggling readers, nor should it be the only focal point of early reading instruction. In addition to phonemic awareness, phonics, vocabulary, fluency, and comprehension are also vital components of effective reading programs. Using research-based strategies in all of these instructional areas helps establish effective literacy learning for young students.

Today, educators interested in implementing effective phonemic awareness instruction in their classrooms may need specific information about this important early reading component: What is phonemic awareness? Why is it important? What does research say about how phonemic awareness instruction can be used most effectively? This chapter will address these questions and will highlight the findings from key scientific research that supports each response.

What Is Phonemic Awareness?

Phonemic awareness is the ability to focus on and manipulate the spoken sounds of language in order to produce spoken words. *Phonemes* are the smallest units of speech that affect the meaning of words. Children who have acquired phonemic awareness can, for example, tell you that changing /b/ in the word *bat* to /k/ changes the word from *bat* to *cat*, or that the word *dog* is formed by combining the three sounds or phonemes /d/ /o/ /g/. A phoneme signals a difference in meaning to a listener who knows the language.

Phonemes are combined to form syllables and words. Phonemes, however, do not necessarily correspond to the number of letters in a word. Some words, such as *oh*, contain just one phoneme. Most words contain a blend of phonemes. The word *do*, for example, contains two phonemes; the word *check* contains three phonemes; the word *drop* contains four phonemes.

Phonemic Awareness, Phonological Awareness, and Phonics: What's the Difference?

Phonemic awareness, although related to phonological awareness and phonics, is different from either of those concepts. *Phonological awareness* encompasses an understanding of larger units of sounds in spoken language, such as syllables, onsets, and rimes, in addition to phonemes. Phonological awareness includes an awareness of sound units such as words within sentences, syllables within words, and phonemes within syllables and words (Opitz, 2000).

Phonics, by contrast, focuses on connecting the sounds of language to the symbols or printed letters that are used to represent those sounds. A child can display his or her knowledge of phonics by identifying, for example, that the letter *c* that makes the first sound (/k/) in *cat* or that the letter *l* makes the last sound in *ball*.

Why Is Phonemic Awareness Important?

A compelling research base exists to support the relationship between phonemic awareness and reading acquisition (IRA, 1998). Early studies of phonemic awareness, such as those conducted by Shankweiler and Liberman (1972), explained that spoken words could not simply be analyzed by phonological segments: Those segments had to be broken down further according to the discrete phonemes that comprised word segments. These researchers were among the first to

4
....

CHAPTER 1

*Phonemic
Awareness:
What Does
Research Tell Us?*

suggest that the inability to distinguish word segments was at the root of many reading problems.

Further studies found that the ability to distinguish one phoneme from another was not a "hard-wired" aspect of speech and language processing; children do not automatically or instinctively acquire phonemic awareness. Rather, phonemic awareness emerged as a result of experience and interactions with spoken language (Ferguson, 1986; Lindblom, 1992). Although children may possess the ability to produce phonemes from infancy, they are not able to consciously manipulate those phonemes without experience and exposure to language use.

Evidence suggests that phonemic awareness is strongly related to success in both reading and spelling (Ball & Blachman, 1991; Liberman, Shankweiler, Fischer, & Carter, 1974; Treiman & Baron, 1983). According to the report of the National Reading Panel (2000), studies have identified phonemic awareness and letter knowledge as the two best predictors of how well children will learn to read during their first two years in school.

Share, Jorm, Maclean, and Matthews (1984) assessed kindergartners on several factors as they entered school. Those factors included phonemic segmentation, letter-name knowledge, memory for sentences, vocabulary, father's occupational status, parental reports of reading to children, and television viewing habits. Over the next two years, the researchers continued to follow the same group of students and examined which factor among those studied best predicted how well the children were reading in first and second grades. The researchers found that phonemic awareness, along with letter knowledge, were the top predictors of children's future reading achievement.

Other studies have found phonemic awareness to be not only a strong predictor of future reading success but also a necessary prerequisite for becoming a successful reader (Bradley & Bryant, 1983; Tunmer, Herriman, & Nesdale, 1988). A comprehensive survey of reading research found that children who lacked phonemic awareness were "severely handicapped in their ability to master print" (Adams, 1990, p. 412). In addition, Juel (1988) found that children lacking phonemic awareness in first grade were more likely to have reading difficulties in fourth grade. However, as children's knowledge of the unique characteristics of different phonemes increases, so too does their ability to recognize and manipulate the individual phonemes in words (Torgesen & Burgess, 1998).

How Can I Help Students Acquire Phonemic Awareness?

Many children need explicit, systematic phonemic awareness instruction in order to become aware of the patterns they hear in spoken language. Research documented in the *Report of the National Reading Panel* (National Reading Panel, 2000) indicates that the benefits of phonemic awareness instruction were greater under three specific conditions. Phonemic awareness instruction was found to be most effective when:

1. Children received focused and explicit instruction on one or two phonemic awareness skills as opposed to being taught a combination of three or more phonemic awareness skills.
2. Phonemic manipulation was taught using printed letters of the alphabet.
3. Instruction occurred in small groups as opposed to individually or in a large group.

These implications remind educators of the interrelationship between phonemic awareness and the alphabetic principle that is typically associated with phonics instruction. Although phonemic awareness focuses on manipulating the sound system of language, it is not entirely disconnected from letters, print, and phonics. Phonemic awareness growth results when the use of print is combined with phonemic awareness instruction. Research also suggests that phonemic awareness instruction is most effective when it is combined with print awareness. Incorporating the use of print and letters with phonemic awareness instruction enhances the effectiveness of phonemic awareness instruction and encourages students to become more active participants in phonemic awareness activities (Calfee, 1998).

Who Benefits from Phonemic Awareness Instruction?

The benefits of phonemic awareness instruction have been documented for a wide variety of students. Those students include the following:

- Children in preschool, prekindergarten, and kindergarten showed greater gains following phonemic awareness instruction than children in first grade and above.

- Children learning to read English showed greater gains than children learning to read in other alphabetic languages.
- Children from both low and mid-to-high socioeconomic status (SES) backgrounds benefited similarly from phonemic awareness instruction.
- Phonemic awareness instruction helps all types of children improve their reading, including normally developing readers, at-risk students, readers with disabilities, children across various SES levels, children learning to read English, and children from preschool grades through sixth grade.

Are There Stages of Phonemic Awareness Development? Is There a Particular Order in Which Phonemic Awareness Skills Should Be Learned?

Researchers have not identified an exact sequence of phonemic awareness skill development, but they have found that some phonemic awareness tasks require a more sophisticated understanding of the language sound structure than others (IRA, 1998). For example, older infants and toddlers often exhibit some ability to process information about sound segments; however, their ability to do so is not yet well developed (Metsala & Walley, 1998). Similarly, most children are able to identify and produce rhyming words before they are able to segment words according to the phonemes that they hear when the words are spoken.

Listed here, from the simplest to the most challenging, are common types of phonemic awareness tasks. These types of tasks can be used to assess a child's phonemic awareness development and to provide a framework for the kind of instruction the child will need in order to move forward in developing phonemic awareness:

1. *Phoneme isolation.* The child can recognize the individual sounds in words. For example, if the teacher asked the child to "Tell me the first sound in *book*," the child would answer /b/.

2. *Phoneme identity.* The child can recognize the common sound in different words. For example, "Tell me the sound that is the same at the beginning of *dad, dog, dip.*" Answer: /d/

3. *Phoneme categorization.* The child can recognize the word with the odd sound in a sequence of three or four words. For exam-

ple, "Which word does not belong in the following set of words: *ran, race, sat, rock?*" Answer: *sat*

4. *Phoneme blending.* The child is able to listen to a sequence of separately spoken sounds and then combine those sounds to form a recognizable word. For example, "If you put the sounds /k/ /a/ /t/ together, what word do they make? Answer: *cat*

5. *Phoneme segmentation.* The child is able to break a word into its sounds by tapping out, counting the sounds, or pronouncing each sound and moving a marker to indicate each individual sound. For example, "How many sounds are there in *chop?*" Answer: three /ch/ /o/ /p/

6. *Phoneme manipulation.* The child is able to delete, add, or substitute phonemes. For phoneme deletion, the child can recognize what word remains when a specified phoneme is removed. For example, "What is *small* without the /s/? Answer: *mall.* For phoneme addition, the child can identify what word is created when a specific phoneme is added. For example, "What is *mall* with /s/ at the beginning? Answer: *small.* For phoneme substitution, the child can recognize a word when one phoneme is replaced by another. For example, "What is *mall* with /t/ instead of /m/?" Answer: *tall.*

What Do These Stages Mean for Classroom Instruction?

The developmental progression of phonemic awareness stages should affect the order and pace in which phonemic awareness skills and corresponding activities are introduced to students in classrooms. The pacing of phonemic awareness instruction should be adapted to meet the needs of developmental levels of students. For example, a student who is at an early stage of phonemic awareness development may benefit from spending more time engaged in simpler, basic phonemic awareness activities. Doing so can provide the student with time to be successful in understanding this important literacy concept as well as ample opportunity to build a solid foundation on which more advanced phonemic awareness concepts can be built.

Lundberg, Frost, and Petersen (1988) observed successful results in kindergarten classrooms when students were engaged in a progression of phonemic awareness activities on a daily basis throughout the school year. In these successful classrooms, children consistently engaged in games and exercises that allowed them to

8
....

CHAPTER 1

*Phonemic
Awareness:
What Does
Research Tell Us?*

attend to sounds in speech and to manipulate those sounds. Dancing, singing, and noncompetitive social games were incorporated into the phonemic awareness instruction. The activities gradually increased in difficulty as the year progressed, and play with spoken language was encouraged as part of a broader literacy program.

The kindergartners observed in the Lundberg study (1988) engaged in a progression of activities. During the first three months of school, children participated in simple listening activities, rhyming exercises, segmenting sentences into words to focus on the length of words in speech, and analyzing the length and sounds of individual words.

By the third month of school, more sophisticated types of phonemic awareness activities were introduced. Children were asked to identify the phonemes in the initial position of words, such as the first sound in *pat*, by stretching the sound out and saying /paaat/. During this time children also practiced adding and removing phonemes from words.

By the fifth month of school, phonemic segmentation and blending were introduced, first with two-phoneme words, and then, on a gradual basis, with longer words. The instructional progression used in these classrooms reflected the research finding that children are generally able to gain control over larger units of sounds before they can gain control over smaller units of sound (Stahl & Murray, 1998).

Other researchers have also suggested that, when selecting words to teach phonemic awareness, teachers begin with those words and phonemes that are easiest to pronounce and manipulate. Ehri and Nunes (2002) offer the following guidelines for determining the ease or difficulty with which certain sounds can be pronounced:

- Words with two phonemes are generally easier to segment than words with three or more phonemes.
- Initial and final phonemes are easier to segment than phonemes in the middle of words.
- Consonant-vowel blends (e.g., /b-o/ in *boat*) are easier to segment than consonant clusters (e.g., /s-t/ in *stand*, /m-p/ in *bump*).
- Certain consonants, called *stop consonants* (e.g., *p, b, t, d, k, g, ch, j*), are more difficult to combine because they are difficult to pronounce without adding the sound of the vowel *uh*. Other consonants, called *continuant consonants* (e.g., *m, n, f, v, s, z, th, sh, l, r*), are generally easier to pronounce because they can be pro-

nounced and held in speech (e.g., *mmm*) without adding the *uh* sound.

When linking these concepts to the use of words, the word *fan*, for example, is relatively easy to pronounce. The word consists of three continuant sounds that can be smoothly blended to form the word *fan*. By contrast, the word *jet* is more difficult to pronounce because sounds pronounced independently of one another must be dropped in order to blend the sounds to form the word *jet* as opposed to *juh–e–tuh*.

Yopp and Yopp (2000) suggest using an instructional sequence that mirrors the general stages of phonemic awareness development:

- *Activities that focus on rhyme.* For example, "Let's think of something that rhymes with *book*." Answer: *look*
- *Activities that focus on syllable units.* For example, "Clap twice for Sarah's name." Answer (Response): /sar/ (clap) – /ah/ (clap)
- *Activities that focus on onset and rime.* For example, "Say just the first part of *blue*." Answer: /bl/
- *Activities that focus on phonemes.* For example, "Let's put these sounds together: /pl/ – /ay/ – /n/." Answer: *plane*

Children may also engage in sound matching, isolation, substitution, blending, segmenting, and deletion tasks using syllables, onsets, rimes, or phonemes. Some activities may be strictly verbal, such as listening to poetry, singing songs, or playing alliteration games that use only spoken language. Other activities may use an auditory cue, such as clapping to the number of syllables in a spoken word. Visual cues, such as blocks or chips, can be used to represent sounds. Engaging in a physical activity, such as hopping as each sound is spoken, can provide children with a kinesthetic cue. Finally, using alphabet letters in combination with speech sounds can link letter cues with phonemic awareness activities.

Based on their own extensive research in the area of phonemic awareness development, Yopp and Yopp (2000) suggest that phonemic awareness instruction for young children should be playful, engaging, and socially interactive. It should stimulate curiosity and experimentation with language in purposeful contexts and should incorporate the use of real reading for authentic purposes. In the next chapter, research-based suggestions for teaching phonemic awareness and specific instructional strategies will be presented.

Professional Development Suggestions

ACED: Analysis, Clarification, Extension, Discussion

I. REFLECTION (10 to 15 minutes)

ANALYSIS:

- What, for you, were the most interesting and/or important ideas in the phonemic awareness introduction and literature review presentation?

  _____

  _____

  _____

  _____

- What information was new to you?

  _____

  _____

  _____

  _____

CLARIFICATION:

- Did anything surprise you? Confuse you?

  _____

  _____

  _____

  _____

EXTENSION:

- What questions do you have?

  _____

  _____

  _____

  _____

II. DISCUSSION (20 minutes)

- Form groups of 4 to 6 members.
- Appoint a *facilitator (timer)* and *recorder*.
- Share responses. Make sure that each person has shared his or her responses to each category (Analysis/Clarification/Extension).
- Help each other with any areas of confusion.
- Answer and/or discuss questions raised by group members.
- On chart paper, the Recorder should summarize the main discussion points and identify issues or questions the group would like to raise for general discussion.

III. APPLICATION (10 minutes)

- Based on your reflection and discussion, how might you apply what you have learned from the phonemic awareness introduction and literature review?

_____

_____

_____

_____

Instructional Strategies for Phonemic Awareness Development

CHAPTER 2

*Instructional
Strategies for
Phonemic
Awareness
Development*

After years of teaching preschool and kindergarten, Mrs. Chapman has come to expect a wide range of developmental levels and literacy foundations among the students in her class. Some children enter school from literacy-rich home environments where they have been immersed in language and books. Others arrive from homes where exposure to literacy and even to the sound system of the English language is limited. Some children seem to absorb language concepts almost effortlessly; others struggle to make even basic connections.

Many children, even those from literacy-rich backgrounds, enter kindergarten lacking phonemic awareness. Most do not realize that words are made up of individual sounds, or phonemes, or even that sentences are made up of individual words (Yopp, 1995). Even fluent speakers produce speech sounds automatically, without paying particular attention to the sounds of the phonemes they use when speaking.

Finding ways to help children develop phonemic awareness so that they can become successful readers is a challenge for teachers like Mrs. Chapman. Fortunately, research has shown that phonemic awareness instruction is possible and that it can contribute to future achievement in reading and in spelling (Ball & Blachman, 1991; Cunningham, 1990). Phonemic awareness has been identified as a significant predictor of a child's reading success in the early years of the formal reading instruction (Adams, Foorman, Lundberg, & Beeler, 1998). For example, when phonemic awareness training was incorporated into Marie Clay's (1985) Reading Recovery program, both the efficiency of the program and the achievement of the students who participated in the program increased (Hatcher, Hulme, & Ellis, 1994; Iversen & Tunmer, 1993).

In order to provide instruction that supports children's phonemic awareness development and to reduce the percentage of students who have not acquired phonemic awareness by the middle of first grade, the International Reading Association's (1998) analysis of research suggests the following:

- Provide opportunities for children to interact within a print-rich environment.
- Provide access to print and opportunities that engage children in using this print in a variety of meaningful contexts as both readers and writers.

- Provide language activities that focus on the form of spoken and written language. In other words, students need to understand both how to articulate sounds in spoken language and how letters are used to represent those sounds. They also need to understand how these sounds and letters can be used to send and receive messages.
- Provide explicit explanations that support their discovery of the alphabetic principle.

Evaluating Your Own Instruction

Before adding new strategies and activities to your instructional repertoire, it is important to evaluate your current teaching practices: What current instructional practices do you find to be effective? What instructional areas need to be fine-tuned? Are there instructional components that are not being covered to the degree that they need to be?

To help you in evaluating your current instructional practices, consider the accompanying semantic feature analysis chart. Along the side of the chart, you will see space for you to list those instructional strategies that you currently use to teach phonemic awareness to your students. These can include activities such as rhyming games, chants and songs, tasks that link phonemic awareness to print, and activities or tasks that mirror the stages of phonemic awareness development discussed in Chapter 1.

Across the top of the chart, you will see components that may be present in the activities that you listed. Of course, not every component can, or should, be part of every activity. Some activities will rely heavily on auditory cues, for example, whereas others may be visual. Some activities will encourage students to interact with classmates; others may invite a more independent response. The key is to seek a balance in terms of the variety of strategies used so that a range of developmental levels and diverse learner needs can be effectively addressed.

Take the time to complete the semantic feature analysis. Place a + sign in the corresponding box for each attribute that is present in a phonemic awareness instructional activity that you currently use. More than one attribute may be present for each activity that you list. You may wish to collaborate with colleagues, as doing so may help you recall the additional phonemic awareness strategies that you use during the course of the school year.

When the semantic feature analysis is complete, it should help you see which aspects of phonemic awareness instruction currently receive a great deal of attention in your classroom and which aspects may not currently receive emphasis. Knowing this will help you to better adjust your instructional routine. Discuss your findings and insights with colleagues.

Semantic Feature Analysis for Current Phonemic Awareness Instructional Practices

Phonemic Awareness Strategies	Auditory	Visual	Kinesthetic	Letter Cue	Interactive	Text-Independent	Text-Connected	Skill Focused

CHAPTER 2

*Instructional
Strategies for
Phonemic
Awareness
Development*

The phonemic awareness strategies described in this section have all been found effective through research. In general, each can be adapted to work successfully with children in grades preK–2. In the descriptions we indicate common procedures and materials, but you should feel free to innovate!

Sound Activities to Match the Developmental Stages of Phonemic Awareness

Purpose:

To provide students with opportunities to play with the sound structure of the English language in ways that correspond to the general stages of phonemic awareness development.

Materials:

A predetermined list of words that will be used for the sound exercises below.

Procedures:

Depending on the student's level of phonemic awareness development, the teacher may select one of the following types of activities. For example, struggling readers or children who are at an earlier stage of phonemic awareness development may benefit from spending more time on simpler activities, such as sound matching, before moving on to more complex activities. As students' knowledge of phonemic awareness increases, teachers may progress to using more sophisticated tasks from this list.

- *Sound matching.* Students are asked to match a word or words with a given sound. For example, the teacher might ask students to think of words that begin with the letter *m*. Sound matching can be extended to middle or ending sounds in words as well as to word families.

- *Sound isolation.* Students are asked to determine the beginning, middle, or ending sound in a word or set of words. For example, the teacher may say three words that begin with the same sound, such as *net, neck, nose,* and ask the students to identify the common sound heard at the beginning of each word (Yopp, 1992).

- *Sound blending.* Students are asked to synthesize (or combine) individual sounds to form a complete word. For example, the teacher might say, "I'm thinking of an animal and here are the sounds in its name /d/, /o/, /g/" (Yopp, 1992). The children should say the word *dog.* An alternative to simply saying the word is to show the children three pictures and ask them to select the picture that represents the sounds that the teacher has spoken.

- *Sound segmentation.* Students are asked to segment each individual sound in a given word. *Dog,* for example, would be segmented into /d/, /o/, /g/. As a variation, students may be asked to segment according to the onset and rime in a given word. For example, the word *stop* would be segmented /st/ and /op/.

- *Sound substitution.* Students are asked to add, subtract, or substitute a sound from an existing word. For example, the teacher may ask, "What word do you get when you take the *s* off *smart?*" The student should reply, "*mart.*" Or the teacher might say, "Add a *p* to *–at.* What word does that make?" The student should reply, "*pat.*"

20

CHAPTER 2

*Instructional
Strategies for
Phonemic
Awareness
Development*

Listening Games

Purpose:

To engage children in listening actively and attentively. This activity is particularly useful for students who are struggling with early literacy concepts and are not yet ready to engage in phonemic awareness activities that use the sound system of the English language. (Adams, Foorman, Lundberg, & Beeler, 1998).

Materials:

No special materials required.

Procedures:

1. Talk with children about how they can listen to different sounds and about the difference between listening with eyes open and with eyes closed.

2. Ask the children to sit with their eyes closed and to listen to the different sounds that they hear. (This step can be repeated by having the children move to a different location—such as outdoors, near the lunchroom, or in the hallway—to listen for sounds that they might discern in different locations.)

3. Ask the children to identify the sounds that they hear while listening attentively. Children may identify sounds such as the following:

breathing	coughing	talking
clock ticking	car horns	clanging
papers rustling	water running	bells ringing

Options:

In order to develop a memory for sounds, students can listen to individual sounds and then try to identify those sounds within a sound sequence. For example, students may close their eyes while the teacher makes a familiar noise, such as the snipping of scissors or the sharpening of a pencil. Children are asked to identify each sound. Then, with their eyes still closed, children listen to two sounds in a row and identify the sounds in the order in which they were heard. With practice, students can listen to and identify a long sound sequence. Additional sounds that can be used for this activity include:

tearing paper   chewing   running a water faucet

closing a window   tapping a foot   writing with a marker

clapping hands   keyboarding   closing a book

CHAPTER 2

*Instructional
Strategies for
Phonemic
Awareness
Development*

Rhyming Games

Purpose:

To familiarize children with the sound structure of the English language through the identification and production of rhyming words.

Materials:

Read-aloud or literature selection that contains several rhyming words.

Procedures:

1. Use the "language-based, focus, and practice" procedure developed by Dugan, Brancato, and Smrekar (2004) for scaffolding phonemic awareness. First, engage the children in a *language-based activity*—for example, reading a story or nursery rhyme, such as "The Old Woman Who Lived in a Shoe."

2. Second, have the children participate in a *focus activity* by having them search for words with specific rimes. Ask them to clap their hands or snap their fingers when they hear these rimes. For example, the first portion of the nursery rhyme reads,

> There was an old woman
> Who lived in a shoe.
> She had so many children
> She didn't know what to do.

Children may snap or clap when they hear *shoe* and *do*.

Option:

Extend the lesson through the use of a *practice* activity in which the children generate or dictate a copy-change story based on the original book that was read to them.

Alliteration Games

23

CHAPTER 2

*Instructional
Strategies for
Phonemic
Awareness
Development*

Purpose:

To enable students to hear and produce alliterations. Doing so will help them to identify sounds that are the same at the beginning of words.

Materials:

A poem or children's literature selection that contains alliteration.

Procedures:

1. To familiarize children with words that start with the same letter, Cunningham (2000) recommends reading a story selection, such as *All about Arthur—An Absolutely Absurd Ape* (Carle, 1975), that utilizes alliteration or tongue twisters.
2. Read the book several times over the course of a week.
3. Point out words that start with the same sound. Ask the children to identify these words with you as you read the book. Children can then try to think of other words that begin with the same sound.

Options:

As an extension activity, children can create alliteration phrases or sentences using their own names and the sounds that begin their names. For example:

Bob bought a bike.
Mark made macaroni.
Sarah sang a silly song.

24

CHAPTER 2

*Instructional
Strategies for
Phonemic
Awareness
Development*

Sound Boxes

Purpose:

To provide a concrete tool for students to use when segmenting sounds. Sounds boxes (Elkonin, 1973) have been found to be particularly useful for children who struggle with identifying and segmenting sounds (Clay, 1985).

Materials:

- Sound boxes (as illustrated)
- Chips or markers for students to place in each of the sound box squares
- Picture cards or a list of words that will be said aloud to the child

Procedures:

1. Place a drawing or card containing a series of boxes (see illustration) in front of the child.
2. Show the child a picture of an object or say a word to the child— for example *cake*. Ask the child to repeat the word and to "stretch out" or segment the sounds that he or she hears in that word.
3. Ask the child to push a chip into each box as he or she says each part of the word, for example, *c – a – k*. It is important to note that the boxes represent the sounds in words, not the number of letters. *Cake*, for example, has three sounds but four letters.

Options:

Once the child gains competency in segmenting words containing three sounds, he or she can progress to words containing four sounds, such as *track, crush,* and *pest.*

26
....
CHAPTER 2

*Instructional
Strategies for
Phonemic
Awareness
Development*

Reading Predictable Texts

Purpose:

To engage children in the shared reading of predictable books for the purpose of allowing children to interact with repeated text patterns, refrains, and rhymes.

Materials:

A big book or predictable text that is visually accessible to all the students hearing the story.

Procedures:

1. Read the book to the children so that they can see the print and pictures as you are reading the story.
2. Reread the story, encouraging the children to join the reading, perhaps by reading the story's refrain or echo reading sections of the book. (In echo reading, you read a line and the children repeat it.)
3. Students can be asked to identify words that begin with or contain a given sound. For example, in the big book *Mrs. Wishy Washy* (Crowley, 1990) words such as *wishy*, *washy*, and *well* begin with *w*.
4. Students might also look for the number of times a key word is used in a sentence or in the story, or the number of rimes they can find on a page of text.

Options:

Children can act out the story; use sentence strips to highlight key words; and compare and contrast the letters, rimes, and words in the text.

Text Play and Writing (Hinky Pinkies)

Purpose:

To develop sound awareness by identifying and/or constructing simple riddles and rhymes.

Materials:

No special materials required.

Procedures:

Develop Hinky Pinkies by first identifying a rhyming word pair that could be an answer to a riddle. For example, *soggy doggy* could be the answer to the riddle, *"What is another name for a wet puppy?"*

Options:

Hinky Pinkies can be altered to include alliteration. To do this, the answer to the riddle should contain two or more words, each beginning with the same letter. Teacher Patricia Watson suggested the following examples:

What do you call a band that is not allowed to play? A banned band.

What is another name for a bear without its fur? A bare bear.

What do you call a sweet doe? A dear deer.

What do you call a very neat instructor? A tidy teacher.

What do you call a dog that weighs 16 ounces? A pound puppy.

What do you call a dog that fits in your hand? A palm puppy.

28
....

CHAPTER 2

*Instructional
Strategies for
Phonemic
Awareness
Development*

Making Concrete Connections between Sounds and Letters (Predictable Charts)

Purpose:

To use children's own experiences and insights to make explicit connections between sounds and letters. Predictable charts help students to make explicit letter–sound connections, learn high-frequency words, apply concepts of print, and write authentic text that can be used as tools for both reading and skill building (Hall & Williams, 2001).

Materials:

- A read-aloud book, such as *When Autumn Comes* (Maass, 1992) or *Apples and Pumpkins* (Rockwell, 1989)
- Lined chart paper
- One sheet of 18″ × 24″ construction paper for each child
- Glue
- Scissors

Procedures:

1. Read the story or stories.
2. Discuss the story; relate it to the students' own experiences.
3. Using the story *When Autumn Comes* or *Apples and Pumpkins* as an example, explain to the children that they are going to take an "autumn walk" to look for different signs of the changing season, such as those described in the books.
4. After taking an autumn walk together as a class, tell one object or sign of autumn that you saw while walking. For example, "I see red leaves."
5. Explain to the students that they will be creating a chart that tells about their autumn walk. Model the first sentence for the children using the stem sentence, "I see. . . ." Introduce key words as you write them on the chart paper in front of the children. For example, you may introduce the word *see* by asking the children what sound is heard at the beginning of the word, and then spelling each letter in the word.

29

CHAPTER 2
*Instructional
Strategies for
Phonemic
Awareness
Development*

6. Ask the children to dictate their sentences using your model. Write each sentence on the chart, putting each child's name after his or her contribution. (Given the short attention span of emergent readers, the dictation of sentences may be broken up into two or three different sessions.)

7. The next day, have each child read his or her own sentence to the class as you point to each word. Discuss concepts such as sounds, letters, words, and similarities and differences between sentences.

8. Make a class big book. Once each student has had a chance to read his or her sentence from the chart paper, cut the sentences from the chart, and have each child paste his or her sentence onto a piece of construction paper. Each child will draw a picture at the top of the paper to illustrate the sentence.

9. Combine the paper pages, add a book cover, and create a big book that can become part of the classroom library.

Option:

Students can bring in photographs of family celebrations, trips, or family members. Each student then provides a sentence that describes what is happening in the photo he or she has selected. You record the responses on chart paper.

30

CHAPTER 2

*Instructional
Strategies for
Phonemic
Awareness
Development*

Making Connections to Phonological Awareness

Knowledge of phonemic awareness can be used as a foundation for phonological awareness development. Opitz (2000) offers the following suggestions, which can be used to enhance both phonemic awareness and phonological awareness:

- *Embed phonemic and phonological awareness into everyday reading and writing experiences.* Classroom literacy routines, such as read-alouds, shared reading, guided reading, independent reading, modeled writing, interactive writing, and independent writing, can all provide opportunities for presenting and reviewing concepts connected to the sound system of language.

- *Provide time for young children to write using invented spelling.* Invented spelling can provide an outlet through which children can apply their growing knowledge of sound–symbol (letter) relationships. By reading a student's invented spelling, you can assess the degree to which a child's understanding of the sound system of language is developing. That knowledge can be used to inform instructional decisions about the use of strategies that would benefit the child.

- *Read aloud children's literature that focuses on specific language features.* Literature that emphasizes a particular aspect of language such as rhyme, alliteration, phoneme substitution, or phoneme segmentation can provide a springboard for listening to, talking about, and playing with language sounds.

- *Use fun, engaging oral language activities.* Use activities that are extensions of literature. Phonemic awareness should not be addressed through drill-type activities. It can and should be a meaningful part of literacy experiences that occur throughout the school day.

- *Determine what students need.* Rather than randomly using sound-language activities, assess where the children are in terms of their understanding of the language sound system. Use that assessment to determine what they need to learn next in order to progress as emerging readers.

- *Involve families.* Parents are not always sure about how or what to do to help. Rather than providing parents with a lengthy book or idea list, provide information gradually. For example, you might select a particular story and then offer a brief explanation of how to read the story with a child, so that phonemic and phonological awareness concepts can be reinforced.

Acquiring phonemic awareness is a means rather than an end. Phonemic awareness should be included as part of a total literacy program in order to help students understand and use the alphabetic system to read and write. Phonemic awareness instruction does not constitute a complete reading program. It is, however, a critical foundational piece on which further literacy development can be built. When children enter school, they differ in their phonemic awareness development. Many will benefit from systematic, thoughtful instruction that allows them opportunities to learn both the skills needed for future literacy engagement as well as how those skills can be applied to purposeful reading and writing. There is no "one right" phonemic awareness program that can magically solve all literacy concerns. Instead, you need to consider the diverse needs of your students when selecting a phonemic awareness program or phonemic awareness instructional methods. Evidence-based strategies and instructional guidelines, such as those discussed in this chapter, can help provide you with direction for effective phonemic awareness instruction.

31

CHAPTER 2
*Instructional
Strategies for
Phonemic
Awareness
Development*

Phonemic Awareness Materials and Programs

Materials for phonemic awareness instruction and practice are abundant. Numerous children's book titles, as well as Web resources, are suggested in Chapter 5. These are a treasure trove of enjoyable poetry, songs, and rhymes that can be used to support children's phonemic awareness development. Commercial programs that focus on phonemic awareness are also available. In evaluating these, we recommend that you focus on the following questions:

- Is the program based on an accurate definition of phonemic awareness?
- Is the program intended for a range of developmental levels?
- Will children find the activities engaging?
- Is the amount of time per day appropriate? Are suggested phonemic awareness activities taught in small increments, consistently, over time?
- Is the overall instructional routine appropriate?
- Are a variety of scaffolding practices available for children who need it?
- Is skill instruction connected to authentic texts?
- Are assessment ideas offered?

Professional Development Suggestions

Phonemic Awareness and Phonics

- How can poetry help you help children learn about onsets, rimes, rhymes, and other issues related to phonemic awareness? Work together to develop some phonemic awareness routines that involve poetry.

  _____

  _____

  _____

  _____

  _____

- How much word study instruction should be whole-group oriented? How much should be small-group oriented? What kinds of groups should be formed? How much individual work should be assigned? And for all of these questions, why?

  _____

  _____

  _____

  _____

  _____

- Revisit the semantic feature analysis on current phonemic awareness instructional practices that you completed at the beginning of the chapter. Now, consider the strategies presented in this chapter as well as discussions you may have had with colleagues about phonemic awareness strategies. How might you adjust your semantic feature analysis to include new strategies and ideas that you may implement in your classroom? Revise your semantic feature analysis and then discuss the instructional changes you will make with your colleagues.

  _____

  _____

  _____

  _____

  _____

CHAPTER 3

Assessing Phonemic Awareness Development

Big Ideas

In each of the books in this series, we have identified several "big ideas" to guide your thinking about assessment. These big ideas apply to assessing all aspects of literacy learning (indeed, to all learning), but the comments and examples below frame them in the context of assessing children's understanding related to phonemic awareness.

- *Focus on critical information.* Aim for a direct connection between what you need to know and the assessment tools/strategies you use. You can decide about critical information by considering the broad definition of phonemic awareness presented earlier in this book. In general, your assessment plans should allow you to find out how well children understand the concept of phonemes and can identify and manipulate (e.g., blend, segment, delete, substitute) phonemes. It may also help to think about a student whose phonemic awareness abilities are very strong. Try making a list of observable indicators: What would he or she do? Say? What would you see or hear that shows strengths in phonemic awareness? Having thought about the abstract definition and your own students, you can then decide on critical information. McTighe and Wiggins (2004) suggest that this process works best when it begins at the end: (1) if the desired result is for learners to _____, (2) then assessment should provide you with evidence of _____, (3) and so assessment tasks need to include something like _____.

- *Look for patterns of behavior.* Rob Tierney (1998) notes that assessment "should be viewed as ongoing and suggestive, rather than fixed or definitive" (p. 385). No one instance can possibly tell you what you need to know about a child's phonemic awareness. Tasks can certainly affect children's abilities to show what they know, for example. So, your goal should be to determine patterns of behavior that show phonemic awareness abilities. To do this, you need a plan. Get baseline information about children at the beginning of the year. Then select a few children on which to focus each week. Some of this will be routine, but you may also want to select children about whom you need more information or children whose current behavior is surprising in some way (Rasinski & Padak, 2004).

- *Recognize developmental progressions (can't, can sometimes, can always) and attend to children's cultural or linguistic differences.* Tierney (1998) advises that "assessment should be more developmental and sustained than piecemeal and shortsighted" (p. 384). "I envision . . . assessments that build upon, recognize, and value rather than displace what students have experienced in their worlds" (p. 381). Your plans should be sensitive to both of these issues. Developmental progressions in phonemic awareness may, for example, mean that children can recognize some aspect (e.g., rhyming) before they can independently produce it. Moreover, this approach to assessment will allow you to reduce the number of children who need to be assessed over the course of the school year. When you are certain that a child has developed awareness of or ability in some aspect of interest (e.g., blending), you will no longer need to assess that child in that domain. Good record-keeping will enable you to keep assessments streamlined and focused on children about whom you have questions. Cultural or linguistic differences may influence some aspects of children's phonemic awareness performance. Children who are learning English, for example, may have first language phonology that differs from English, and this can affect their performance on assessment tasks. Knowing about these differences can help ensure that your assessments yield useful information.

• *Be parsimonious.* The question: How much assessment information do you need? The answer: Enough to help you make good instructional decisions. One way to conceptualize this quantity-of-information question is to think in terms of three related layers of assessment information.

All Students

Some Students
Struggling readers benefit from additional in-class assessment.

A Few Students
Challenged readers require assessment outside the classroom.

Source: Rasinski and Padak (2004, p. 277). Reprinted by permission of Pearson Education, Inc.

At the top of the figure is what is done for and with all students in the class. Begin with a broad plan to assess children's phonemic awareness at the beginning of the year and then, perhaps, reassess quarterly. Remember that you probably won't need to assess all children as the school year progresses because some will already have demonstrated their phonemic awareness ability. Then think about results—what (or whom) do you still have questions about? This is the point to move to the second layer of the triangle. Here, you will do more focused (and time-consuming) phonemic awareness assessments. You might work individually with a child, perhaps more of what you've already done or a "deeper" assessment. If you still have questions, don't hesitate to ask for outside help. A child or two in the class may benefit from a diagnosis by a reading specialist or other highly specialized professional. Don't delay and don't hesitate. Every lost day represents lost opportunities for that child's learning. Above all, keep assessments at these different layers related to one another, focused on the same key issues.

• *Use instructional situations for assessment purposes.* Tierney (1998) notes that, ideally, "assessments should emerge from the classroom rather than be imposed upon it" (p. 375). We can think of two good reasons for this stance, one conceptual and the other practical. From a conceptual perspective, you want to know how children behave in typical instructional situations. After all, a major purpose of assessment is to provide instructional guidance. From a practical standpoint, gathering assessment information from instruction saves time for your teaching and children's learning. Children don't learn much of value during testing sessions. To evaluate your phonemic awareness instruction for possible assessment situations, you might begin by listing instructional routines that focus on phonemic awareness—when and how do you ordinarily work with children on issues related to phonemic awareness? The semantic feature analysis chart that you developed in Chapter 2 may help you with this. Then develop a plan to capture observations about what children know and can do during instruction. This may be as simple as preparing an observation chart (see next page) for making brief notes. Above all, take Karen West's (1998) advice to heart: "I want instruction and evaluation to be in meaningful authentic contexts" (p. 550).

• *Include plans for (1) using assessment information to guide instruction and (2) sharing assessment information with children and parents.* The last step of your assessment planning might be to double-check ideas against their primary purpose: to help you teach more effectively. You will also want to think about how to share assessment information with your students and their parents. With regard to the former, it may be particularly important to think about how you can adjust instruction for both children who need more work with phonemic awareness and children who have mastered these concepts and are ready for different instruction. Grouping for instruction will probably be necessary, so you will want to think about the management issues associated with particular grouping patterns for young children. Moreover, consider how you can share assessment information with children and their parents. Knowing that they are making progress will keep children engaged in their learning. And parents, of course, are both interested in their children's progress in school and frequently willing to assist in their children's education. Indeed, many phonemic awareness activities are gamelike and therefore perfect additions to at-home suggestions for parents. Rob Tierney (1998) reminds us that it is important to keep parents informed, but more than that, involved: "Rather than keep the parent or caregiver at arm's length . . . , we need to embrace the concerns that parents have and the contributions they can make" (p. 380).

Evaluate Your Current Assessment Practices

The accompanying chart may help you take a careful look at your current assessment practices in phonemic awareness. To complete the chart, first list all the ways you currently assess students' phonemic awareness in the "Assessment Tool/ Strategy" column. Then consider the information each tool or strategy provides about each of the critical aspects by marking the chart: + = excellent source of information; − = some information; blank = no information. When the chart is complete, make plans for revision. Are some critical aspects receiving too much/not enough attention? Can some tools/strategies be eliminated or revised? What revisions will enhance your overall assessment strategies?

Critical Aspects: Phonemic Awareness

Assessment Tool/Strategy	Rhyming	Phoneme Identity	Blending/ Segmenting	Deleting/ Substituting

Notes about revisions:

_____

_____

_____

_____

Ideas for Assessment

What did you conclude by analyzing your current strategies for assessing phonemic awareness? Perhaps you are satisfied that you have enough of the right kind of information about your students. If not, you may find some of the following ideas helpful for supplementing your plans.

Observation Chart

You can duplicate a chart like the one on the next page to use at times when children show their phonemic awareness abilities. You can make brief notes on the chart or use some kind of symbol system, such as O = Outstanding, S = Satisfactory, and U = Unsatisfactory. Since assessing children in this way once every month or two may provide enough information, you can focus on different students each week and, over time, observe all your students.

Observation Chart

Aspects	Rhyming	Phoneme Identity	Blending/Segmenting	Deleting/Substituting
Child's Name				
Child's Name				
Child's Name				
Child's Name				

Rhyming

Two rhyming tasks are outlined here. If children are able to complete 8 out of 10 of these successfully, you can judge their abilities strong in these areas.

1. For rhyme recognition, say the sets of words below. Ask the child to raise a hand (or clap) if the words rhyme:

   nice   grow   bed   lace   jack   he   meet   mop   cat   to
   mice   slow   bad   face   black   tree   might   top   hat   tap

2. For rhyme production, say the first word for the child and ask him or her to say another word that rhymes. You may want to make this into a game: "I will say a word. You say one that rhymes. For example, if I say *bat,* you could say *sat.* What if I said *back?* What could you say?"

Phoneme Isolation/Identification

To informally assess phoneme isolation, use the first word in each group. Ask the child to tell you the first (or last) sound in the word. To informally assess phoneme identification, use the entire groups of words. Ask the child to tell you what sound is the same in the words. If children are able to complete 8 out of 10 of these successfully, you can judge their abilities strong in these areas.

cat	me	dock	mop	bed
cake	free	sock	Mary	ball
carry	tree	lock	mud	big
fun	play	hit	son	jam
fan	stay	bit	silly	jump
fire	away	sit	sand	jiggle

Phoneme Segmentation/Blending

To informally assess segmentation, ask the child to tell you the sounds that make up these words (from Rasinski & Padak, 2001, p. 34). To informally assess blending, you say the sounds and ask the child to tell you the word. For either task, you may want to provide some practice, perhaps using *lock* and *flap* before beginning. If children are able to complete 8 out of 10 of these successfully, you can judge their abilities strong in these areas.

| to | me | fight | low | he | vain | is | am | be | meet | jack |
| dock | lace | mop | this | jot | grow | nice | cat | show | bed | stay |

Plans for Change

In this chapter, you have evaluated your own assessment strategies for phonemic awareness and, as a result, perhaps generated some ideas for change. Use the accompanying chart on page 47 to make notes about the changes you wish to make. As you do so, make sure that these changes reflect the "big ideas" outlined at the beginning of the chapter:

- Focus on critical information.
- Look for patterns of behavior.
- Recognize developmental progressions and attend to children's cultural or linguistic differences.
- Be parsimonious. (Which of your strategies will work for all of your students? Which might be reserved for more careful attention to some students' phonemic awareness abilities?)
- Use instructional situations for assessment purposes.
- Include plans for (1) using assessment information to guide instruction and (2) sharing assessment information with children and parents.

You may want to share your plans with others to get their feedback.

Professional Development Suggestions

Book Club

Although you have taught kindergarten for years, this is your first year in this school system. In your previous school, few children had adequate phonemic awareness when they began kindergarten, so you and the children spent a few minutes each day on phonemic awareness. You begin the year with this assumption about kindergartners in this new school as well.

Children's responses to the phonemic awareness activities soon convince you that your assumptions about their needs were wrong. In contrast to the children at your previous school, a significant portion of your current kindergartners appear to know the basics of phonemic awareness—they can isolate beginning sounds, many understand the concept of rhyming, and a few appear able to blend sounds together.

QUESTIONS

- What assumptions about children's phonemic awareness should teachers make? Why?

  _____

  _____

  _____

  _____

- What kinds of diagnostic assessments for phonemic awareness make sense for kindergartners?

  _____

  _____

  _____

  _____

- How can teachers use the results of the diagnostic assessments to plan instruction for young children?

  _____

  _____

  _____

  _____

- Is there any harm in involving children in phonemic awareness activities that focus on concepts they appear to have mastered? Why?

_____

_____

_____

_____

Reflection Protocol

ACED: Analysis, Clarification, Extension, Discussion

REFLECTION (10 to 15 minutes)

ANALYSIS:

- What, for you, were the most interesting and/or important ideas in this chapter?

_____

_____

_____

_____

- What information was new to you?

_____

_____

_____

_____

CLARIFICATION:

- Did anything surprise you? Confuse you?

_____

_____

_____

_____

EXTENSION:

- What questions do you have?

_____

_____

_____

_____

DISCUSSION (30 minutes)

- Form groups of 4 to 6 members.
- Appoint a *facilitator (timer)* and *recorder.*
- Share responses. Make sure that each person has shared his or her responses to each category (Analysis/Clarification/Extension).
- Help each other with any areas of confusion.
- Answer and/or discuss questions raised by group members.
- On chart paper, the Recorder should summarize the main discussion points and identify issues or questions the group would like to raise for general discussion.

APPLICATION (10 minutes)

- Based on your reflection and discussion, how might you apply what you have learned from this chapter?

_____

_____

_____

_____

Curriculum Alignment

Component	What Is. . .	What Should Be. . .
Curriculum		
Instruction		
Materials		
Assessment		
Home Connection		

Source: Adapted from Taylor and Collins (2003).

CHAPTER 4

Fostering Home–School Connections

Research tells us that when children understand how the sounds of spoken language are blended together to create words, their capacity to learn how to read improves. The best way for children to learn about how the sound system of language works is to play with the sounds. Research has also shown that phonemic awareness development in young children is related to home experiences, including being read to, engaging in language games, and having early writing experiences, all of which encourage the child to interact with language and print.

It is important for teachers to understand, and to explain to parents, the developmental nature of phonemic awareness growth—that all children may not be developmentally ready to engage in all types of phonemic awareness activities at the same point on the calendar. Parents should also understand that it is best to begin by modeling and using simpler phonemic awareness activities and then progressing to more sophisticated activities as the child is ready to succeed at them.

The following ideas are suggested ways to foster phonemic awareness development. These activities can be used during classroom instruction and can be suggested to families as ways to support a child's phonemic awareness development at home (Day, Dommer, Mraz, & Padak, 2002):

- Sing simple songs with the child; say nursery rhymes together. This works particularly well if the stories or rhymes are short. Stress the rhyming words, for example:

    Hickory Dickory DOCK
    The mouse ran up the CLOCK

- Look for books in the library or in bookstores that have rhyming words. A children's librarian can help you to locate good books. Read these with the child. Emphasize the rhyming words.

- Use a picture dictionary. Look at the pages with the child. Ask the child to point to objects on the page that begin with letters you say. For example, you could say, "Can you find something on the page that starts with /d/?" Or, you could point to something on the page and ask the child, "What sound does this begin with?" or "Does this begin with /d/?"

- Play "Sound Scavenger Hunt." (In the classroom, this works well during transition times as a way of dismissing students from a large group one by one. At home, this works well in the car.) For example, say, "Let's find something that begins with the sound /s/" or "I see a pencil. What sound does *pencil* begin with?" When the child can find beginning sounds easily, the same game can be played with ending sounds.

- Play rhyming word games. Ask the child to listen to pairs of words. If the word pairs rhyme, ask the child to clap or to sit down or to jump up. For example, say, "cat, fat" "cat, dog" or "dog, fog."

- Play "I Say." Use this frame to play with words. You say one simple word. The child says another word that rhymes:

  "I say *bat*. You say _____."
  "I say *tree*. You say _____."

- Collect pictures from magazines, newspapers, or junk mail. Ask the child to find things in the pictures that begin with certain sounds. For example, you might ask the child to find things that begin with /p/. The child could make a sound book by cutting these pictures out and pasting them in a homemade book (scrapbook). The book may become part of the child's home library.

- Using the same magazines, newspapers, and junk mail, cut out some pictures. Give three of them to the child, two that begin with the same sound and one that does not. Ask the child to find the one picture that does not belong.

- Play "Change the Word." Give the child a simple word. Ask him or her to change the beginning sound of the word to make a new word. For example, you could say, "My word is *boat*. Change /b/ to /k/. What is your word?"

- Play "Walk and Talk." Using initial consonant sounds, find items in the neighborhood or within the home that begin with selected sounds.

- Make "Phono Cards" by drawing illustrations of words families, such as *mat, bat, cat, hat,* and *rat* for the -at family.

- Use family photographs to practice identifying letters and sounds.

- Play "Match Magic." Choose words from books, magazines, or newspapers whose beginning and ending letters match. Draw pictures illustrating these words.

- Play "Pick-a-Picture." Pick pictures that have the same beginning and ending sounds. Create a collage with these pictures.

Engaging Families in Home Literacy Activities

The importance of parental involvement in children's early reading is widely recognized by researchers and practitioners. Children whose families encourage at-home literacy activities have higher phonemic awareness and decoding skills (Burgess, 1999), higher reading achievement in the elementary grades (Cooter, Marrin, & Mills-House, 1999), and advanced oral language development (Senechal, LeFevre, & Thomas, 1998). Family literacy professionals often point out that parents are their children's first and most important teachers, yet many parents remain unfamiliar with young children's developmental progression toward proficiency as readers and writers. Other parents may want to do *something* at home to help their children succeed as emergent readers and writers, but they are unfamiliar with exactly *what* to do to support that growth. Instructing parents to simply "read to your child" may be a start, but it is not enough. Parents need specific suggestions and guidelines about what to do and how to respond to their child's literacy development.

In *Literacy Tips for Children*, Mraz, Padak, and Baycich (2002) offer suggestions to parents on what to look for in terms of emergent literacy development at different stages in a child's life, suggestions on how families can help to support literacy development at each stage, and types of books that are appealing to children at different developmental stages. Those suggestions are summarized here.*

Literacy Tips for Children Ages 0–3 Years Old

What to Look For

From birth to 8 months, a baby will

- React to your voice
- Laugh and babble
- Make noises to show interest and to get your attention
- Learn to understand names of common people and things

---

*Reprinted with permission, Ohio Literacy Resource Center, http://literacy.kent.edu.

From 8 months to 18 months (1½ years), a baby

- May be able to say two or three words
- Will babble in long strings that sound like sentences
- Can understand many words
- Will make noises to get help or to get your attention
- Will look at picture books with you

Toddlers (18 months to 3 years)

- May be able to say 200 different words
- Will put words together in simple sentences
- Will know the names of many common things in the house
- Will enjoy listening to stories for short periods of time

How Families Can Help

- Learning begins with good health. Good food and enough sleep are important for healthy development.
- Spend time with your child. Play with him or her. Include your child in family activities.
- Talk to your child all the time. Sing. Whisper. Make different sounds. Play singing and clapping games.
- Let your child play with toys that have different shapes and that feel different, like teddy bears and pillows.
- Let your child see you reading and writing.
- Teach your child ideas like up–down and in–out. For example, when you swing your child in play, say "Up we go!" "Down we go!"
- Look at picture books with your child. Young children like books with big, bold pictures. Point to things in the book. When your child starts to talk, ask him or her to find things in the book. For example, "Where is the truck?"

What Kind of Books to Look For (Ages 0–3)

- Cloth or vinyl books that are easy to clean
- Books with bright, simple pictures and patterns
- Board books with thick pages
- Books with familiar objects
- Books with songs or simple stories

- Stories about things that happen in your child's life: going to bed, being a messy eater, missing mom
- Predictable books

Literacy Tips for Children Ages 4–6 Years Old

What to Look For

From ages 4 to 6, look for your child to

- Show an interest in books and ask adults to read to him or her.
- Have favorite books and authors. Your child may ask for favorite books to be read again and again.
- Guess about what will happen in a story. You can help by asking, "What do you think is going to happen?"
- Ask questions about stories, make comments about stories, and connect stories to his or her life.
- Retell or act out stories or parts of stories.
- Pretend to read.
- Learn that we read the print, not the pictures. He or she should begin to look at the print when someone reads a familiar book.
- Scribble or pretend to write. Over time, he or she should begin to use letters. By kindergarten, your child will begin to use sounds to write letters. For example, the word *ball* might be written "B" or "BL."
- Begin to learn the ABCs. By the end of kindergarten, he or she should know all the letters, know some words by sight, and know how to rhyme.

How Families Can Help

- Point out print in everyday life—the cereal box, toys, fast-food restaurants, traffic signals. This helps children learn that print is all around them.
- Sing songs, say little poems or Mother Goose rhymes, and play rhyming word games with your child. Rhyming will become important as children learn to read.
- Tell stories to your child.

- Read aloud to your child. Point to the words on the page. Move your finger from left to right as you read.
- Ask older children to read to younger children.
- Ask your child to read to you (or pretend-read to you). Make this reading an enjoyable time for both you and your child. Don't worry if your child does not read all the words correctly. Make sure your child knows that you think he or she is a capable reader.
- Go to the library together. Check out books together. The librarian can help you find good books for your child.
- Have books, magazines, and newspapers around the house. Let your child see that you like to read.
- Ask your child to write. Ask your child to read the writing to you. Praise your child's efforts. Don't worry about spelling yet.

What Kind of Books to Look For (Ages 4–6)

- Stories that rhyme
- Stories that repeat sentences and words
- Adventures or silly stories
- Books about giants, monsters, dinosaurs, machines, and animals
- Books with poems

Literacy Tips for Children Ages 7–8 Years Old

What to Look For

From ages 7 to 8, look for your child to

- Begin to read. He or she should know some words by sight and figure out other words by sounding them out and checking to see if the guesses make sense.
- Begin to read fluently, with expression and proper phrasing.
- Know about the parts of books. He or she should also know about different types of books, such as fictional stories and non-fictional stories.
- Be able to tell you what he or she has read.

- Read for fun and to learn. He or she should have favorite kinds of books or favorite authors.
- Write notes, sentences, letters, and paragraphs. More words should be spelled correctly. The amount that your child is able to write should increase. You should be able to read what your child has written.

How Families Can Help

- Ask open-ended questions, such as "What do you think?" and "Tell me about that" to help your child become a good problem-solver.
- Make reading and writing something that happens every day in your home. Let your child see you reading and writing. Encourage your child to read and write during free time.
- Visit the public library every week. Help your child get his or her own library card. Help him or her check out books, books on tape, puzzles, and so on.
- Read to your child every day, even after your child learns to read.
- Listen to your child read. Help him or her with tricky words by saying, "Skip it and read to the end of the sentence. Now try again. What makes sense that looks like the word you see?" Tell your child that he or she is a capable reader.
- Play word games, such as thinking of different words to describe the same thing, "Twenty Questions," or "I Spy."
- Support your child's writing. Have writing materials, such as paper, markers, and notebooks, available. Read what your child writes. Tell your child that he or she is a capable writer.
- Limit TV viewing to no more than two hours per day.

What Kinds of Books to Look For (Ages 7–8)

- Books showing how to make things
- Mystery and adventure stories
- Books about collecting things
- Information books

Communicating with Families

Family involvement in early literacy programs has found wide acceptance in professional circles (Purcell-Gates, 2002). Although effective, consistent communication with family members is a critical aspect of any teacher's work, the task can be a daunting one. An effective teacher must seek to develop a collaborative, rather than an adversarial, relationship with parents; convey information about a child's progress in an honest yet supportive manner; suggest home literacy activities to family members; and remain understanding of individual family challenges. To assist in meeting these needs, the following section offers suggestions for preparing, implementing, and extending parent–teacher conferences.

Getting Acquainted

Based on their own school experiences, for some parents the thought of conferencing with a teacher can produce anxiety and the expectation of trouble ahead. Perhaps in their own school days, a request for a conference with a teacher may have signaled to parents and students alike that something was amiss. Or perhaps information about their progress, or lack thereof, as students was conveyed in a condescending or evaluative manner.

Changing the negative expectations that often surround parent–teacher conferences is a challenging but vital endeavor. When parents perceive a teacher to be welcoming, accessible, and responsive to their questions and concerns, a productive rapport can be established. That connection will, in turn, serve to support the child's learning and development.

An information-gathering conference or survey can give parents and teachers the opportunity to become acquainted with one another, to ask questions, and to gather information that will help both parties better understand the needs of the child. Whether presented face to face or through a written survey, the following questions, adapted from Mason and Schumm (2003), can help to guide such communication:

1. What activities does your child enjoy the most at school? At home?

2. How often are you able to read with your child at home?

3. What makes it difficult to read with your child at home?
   - Finding the time
   - Not sure what books to select
   - Too frustrating
   - Not enough books or materials to read
   - Not sure how to help the child when he or she comes to an unfamiliar word
   - Need help reading English

4. Are you able to visit the library with your child? If not, what kind or help or information do you need in order to do so?
   - Information about library locations and hours
   - Information about library procedures
   - Assistance obtaining a library card
   - Assistance selecting appropriate books

5. Which of the following do you find most useful for keeping you informed about school events?
   - Classroom newsletters
   - Parent message board
   - Personal phone calls from the teacher
   - Personal notes from the teacher

6. What would you like me to know about how your child learns?

7. Is there anything else you'd like to share in order for me better understand your child's needs?

Advice for Parent Conferences

Conducting parent–teacher conferences can be both a rewarding and a challenging experience even for the most seasoned of teachers. The following recommendations, adapted from Cooper and Kiger (2005), can help teachers to prepare and implement effective conferences:

- *Schedule an appropriate time for the conference.* Be cognizant of scheduling issues that parents might have. To a reasonable degree, try to offer conference times that coordinate with parents' schedules. For example, conference times may be offered before school, after school, or during the school day if a teacher assistant is available to supervise the class. In some cases, home conferences may be appropriate.

- *Prepare for the conference.* Gather samples of the student's work so that you can illustrate points that you need to make. If additional school personnel need to attend the conference, coordinate their attendance in advance. Make sure that each person knows why he or she is being asked to attend and what he or she will be asked to contribute. Let parents know ahead of time if any support staff members or administrators will be attending the conference. For limited English proficient parents, have a translator available.

- *Select a conference time and location where you will not be interrupted.* Allow adequate time for your presentation at the conference and for parent questions and comments. During the conference, give your full attention to the parents.

- *Conduct the conference in a comfortable, pleasant, professional environment.* Make sure that the room is orderly and inviting. Have comfortable seating available. If possible, hold the conference at a round table.

- *Begin the conference on a positive note.* Point out positive aspects of the child's development and the ways in which the child has progressed.

- *Encourage parents to talk about their concerns.* Often parents come to a conference sharing concerns similar to those that the teacher plans to address. Inviting parents to raise their concerns is usually an effective way to initiate conversation about challenging topics.

- *Listen.* Be empathetic to parents' needs and sincere about finding collaborative solutions to issues that affect the child's learning.

- *Use nontechnical language.* Avoid speaking in "teacher jargon." When you do need to use terms with which parents may not be familiar, try to explain those terms or restate them in a way that will be comprehensible to parents.

- *Give specific suggestions.* Most parents really do want to help their child; however, they may be unsure of what to do or how to help.

- *End your conference with goals.* Make the conclusion of the conference forward-looking. Discuss and agree on goals that you will work on with the child at school as well as goals that can provide learning support at home.

- *Document!* Summarize your agreed-on goals. Write them down. Maintain a record of these goals throughout the school year. The form discussed next is one of many formats that can be used to document important details about the conference.

Conference Record Form

In order to prepare for and document a parent–teacher conference, many teachers find it helpful to use a conference reporting form that allows them to succinctly yet thoroughly record their plans for the conference as well as details of the conference itself.

You may wish to include the following information on a conference record form:

- The student's name
- The date and time of the conference
- The names of the persons attending the conference
- Planned topics of discussion
- Materials and examples of student work products available at the conference
- Notes of main points that were discussed during the conference, including any issues or concerns raised by parents and parents' responses to teacher-raised topics
- Goals agreed on by parents and teachers
- Plans for action or follow-up by both parents and teachers
- The approximate date of the next conference or follow-up communication

Helping parents understand the essential role they play in their children's literacy education and offering them practical suggestions they can use to support children's literacy development are importance steps in establishing productive home–school partnerships. The professional development suggestions offered next invite you to collaborate with colleagues on ways to maintain those partnerships and address challenges that can invariably occur in parent-teacher interactions.

Home–School Connections

1. Working in small groups, discuss your current parent–teacher conferencing practices. What are your biggest conferencing challenges? What questions do parents routinely ask? How do you respond to these questions?

2. Brainstorm additional techniques that teachers could employ to become acquainted with parents at the start of a new school year. Can you think of other questions that could be added to the "getting acquainted survey" presented earlier in this chapter?

3. Working in small groups comprised of both veteran teachers and novice teachers, describe to each another one of your more challenging parent conferences. What made the conference difficult? How did you respond? What did you learn from this experience? Based on what you learned and on what you now know, how might you handle that situation differently if you encountered it at a future conference?

4. In the *Principals' FAQ Project* (Mraz et al., 2001), principals reported that parents' most frequently asked questions about phonemic awareness were as follows:

   - What is phonemic awareness?
   - What's the difference between phonemic awareness and phonics?
   - What's the connection between phonemic awareness and writing?
   - How can I help my child develop phonemic awareness?

   Based on what you have learned through this professional development program, compile responses to each of these frequently asked questions.

CHAPTER 5

Resources

Common Rimes
(Phonograms or Word Families)

ab: tab, drab
ace: race, place
ack: lack, track
act: fact, pact
ad: bad, glad
ade: made, shade
aft: raft, craft
ag: bag, shag
age: page, stage
aid: maid, braid
ail: mail, snail
ain: rain, train
air: hair, stair
ait: bait, trait
ake: take, brake
alk: talk, chalk
all: ball, squall
am: ham, swam
ame: name, blame
amp: camp, clamp
an: man, span
ance: dance, glance
and: land, gland
ane: plane, cane
ang: bang, sprang
ank: bank, plank
ant: pant, chant
ap: nap, snap
ape: tape, drape
ar: car, star
ard: hard, card
are: care, glare
ark, dark, spark
arm: harm, charm

arn: barn, yarn
arp: carp, harp
art: part, start
ase: base, case
ash: cash, flash
ask: mask, task
ass: lass, mass
at: fat, scat
atch: hatch, catch
ate: gate, plate
aught: caught, taught
aw: saw, draw
ave: gave, shave
awn: lawn, fawn
ay: hay, clay
ax: wax, sax
aze: haze, maze
ead: head, bread
eak: leak, sneak
eal: real, squeal
eam: team, stream
ean: mean, lean
eap: heap, leap
ear: year, spear
eat: beat, cheat
eck: peck, check
ed: bed, shed
ee: tee, see
eed: need, speed
eek: leek, seek
eel: feel, knell
eem: deem, seem
een: seen, screen
eep: keep, sheep

eer: beer, peer
eet: feet, sleet
eg: leg, beg
eigh: weigh, sleigh
eight: weight, freight
ell: fell, swell
elt: felt, belt
en: Ben, when
end: tend, send
end: sent, spent
ess: less, bless
et: get, jet
est: rest, chest
ew: flew, chew
ib: bib, crib
ibe: bride, tribe
ice: rice, splice
ick: kick, stick
id: hid, slid
ide: wide, pride
ie: die, pie
ief: thief, chief
ife: wife, knife
iff: cliff, whiff
ift: gift, sift
ig: pig, twig
ight: tight, bright
ike: Mike, spike
ile: mile, tile
ill: fill, chill
ilt: kilt, quilt
im: him, trim
in: tin, spin
ince: since, prince

ind: kind, blind
ine: mine, spine
ing: sing, string
ink: sink, shrink
ip: hip, flip
ipe: ripe, swipe
ire: tire, sire
irt: dirt, shirt
ise: rise, wise
ish: dish, swish
isk: disk, risk
iss: kiss, Swiss
ist: mist, wrist
it: hit, quit
itch: ditch, witch
ite: bite, write
ive: five, hive
ix: fix, six
o: do, to, who
o: go, no, so
oach: coach, poach
oad: road, toad
oal: coal, goal
oam: foam, roam
oan: Joan, loan
oar: boar, roar
oast: boast, coast
oat: boat, float
ob: job, throb
obe: robe, globe
ock: lock, stock
od: rod, sod
ode: code, rode
og: fog, clog
oil: boil, broil
oin: coin, join
oke: woke, spoke

old: gold, scold
ole: hole, stole
oll: droll, roll
ome: dome, home
one: cone, phone
ong: long, wrong
oo: too, zoo
ood: good, hood
ood: food, mood
ook: cook, took
ool: cool, fool
oom: room, bloom
oon: moon, spoon
oop: hoop, snoop
oot: boot, shoot
op: top, chop
ope: hope, slope
orch: porch, torch
ore: bore, snore
ork: cork, fork
orn: horn, thorn
ort: fort, short
oss: boss, gloss
ost: cost, lost
ost: host, most
ot: got, trot
otch: notch, blotch
ote: note, quote
ough: rough, tough
ought: bought, brought
ould: could, would
ounce: bounce, pounce
ound: bound, found
ouse: house, mouse
out: pout, about
outh: mouth, south
ove: cove, grove

ove: dove, love
ow: how, chow
ow: slow, throw
owl: howl, growl
own: down, town
own: known, grown
ox: fox, pox
oy: boy, ploy
ub: cub, shrub
uck: duck, stuck
ud: mud, thud
ude: dude, rude
udge: fudge, judge
ue: sue, blue
uff: puff, stuff
ug: dug, plug
ule: rule, mule
ull: dull, gull
um: sum, chum
umb: numb, thumb
ump: bump, plump
un: run, spun
une: June, tune
ung: hung, flung
unk: sunk, chunk
unt: bunt, hunt
ur: fur, blur
urn: burn, churn
urse: curse, nurse
us: bus, plus
ush: mush, crush
ust: dust, trust
ut: but, shut
ute: lute, flute
y: my dry

Source: From Timothy Rasinki and Nancy D. Padak, *From Phonics to Fluency: Effective Teaching of Decoding and Reading Fluency in the Elementary School,* © 2001. Reprinted by permission of Pearson Education, Inc.

Letter Sounds in Action

Connecting letter sounds to a particular movement or action can be a useful learning tool for children who are kinesthetic learners. The following list, adapted from Cunningham, Moore, Cunningham, and Moore (2004), offers connections between sounds and physical actions.

B: bending, bouncing

C: catching, combing

D: dancing, diving

F: falling, fixing

G: galloping, gasping

H: hopping, hiding, hitting

J: jumping, juggling

K: kicking, kissing

L: laughing, lunging

M: marching, munching

N: napping, nodding

P: punching, painting

R: running, ripping

S: sitting, singing

T: talking, tickling

W: walking, waving

Y: yawning, yelling

Z: zipping, zigzaging

Children's Books for Phonemic Awareness Development

Anastasio, D. (1999). *Pass the peas, please.* Los Angeles, CA: Lowell House.

Baer, G. (1989). *Thump, thump, rat-a-tat-tat.* New York: Harper and Row.

Barrett, J. (2001). *Which witch is which?* New York: Atheneum.

Base, G. (1989). *Animalia.* New York: Harry Abrams.

Bayor, J. (1984). *A: My name is Alice.* New York: Dial.

Bemelmans, L. (1967). *Madeline.* New York: Viking Press.

Benjamin, A. (1987). *Rat-a-tat, pitter pat.* New York: Cromwell.

Berger, S. (2001). *Honk! Toot! Beep!* New York: Cartwheel Books.

Brown, M. W. (1993). *Four fur feet.* New York: Doubleday.

Browne, P. (1996). *A gaggle of geese: The collective names of the animal kingdom.* New York: Atheneum.

Buller, J. (1990). *I love you, good night.* New York: Little Simons.

Butterworth, N. (1990). *Nick Butterworth's book of nursery rhymes.* New York: Viking.

Bynum, J. (2002). *Altoona Baboona.* New York: HarperCollins.

Cameron, P. (1961). *"I can't," said the ant.* New York: Coward-McCann.

Capucilli, A. (2004). *Mrs. McTats and her houseful of cats.* New York: Aladdin.

Cole, J. (1993). *Six sick sheep.* New York: HarperCollins.

dePaola, T. (1985). *Tomie dePaola's mother goose.* New York: Putnam.

deRegniers, B. (1968). *Catch a little fox.* New York: Scholastic.

deRegniers, B., et al. (1988). *Sing a song of popcorn.* New York: Scholastic.

Dodd, L. (2000). *A dragon in a wagon.* Milwaukee, WI: Gareth Stevens.

Eagle, K. (2002). *Rub a dub dub.* Watertown, MA: Charlesbridge.

Ehlert, L. (2001). *Top cat.* New York: HarperCollins.

Eichenberg, F. (1952). *Ape in a cape.* San Diego, CA: Harcourt.

Galdone, P. (1968). *Henny Penny.* New York: Scholastic.

Geisel, T. S. (Dr. Seuss). (1957). *The cat in the hat.* New York: Random House.

Geisel, T. S. (Dr. Seuss). (1960). *Green eggs and ham.* New York: Random House.

Geisel, T. S. (Dr. Seuss). (1963). *Dr. Seuss's ABC.* New York: Random House.

Geisel, T. S. (Dr. Seuss). (1965). *Fox in Socks.* New York: Random House.

Geisel, T. S. (Dr. Seuss). (1965). *Hop on pop.* New York: Random House.

Geisel, T. S. (Dr. Seuss). (1972). *Marvin K. Mooney, will you please go now!* New York: Random House.

Geisel, T. S. (Dr. Seuss). (1974). *There's a wocket in my pocket.* New York: Random House.

Gordon, J. P. (1991). *Six sleepy sheep.* New York: Puffin.

Hennessey, B. G. (1990). *Jake baked the cake.* New York: Viking.

Hoberman, M. A. (1982). *A house is a house for me.* New York: Penguin.

Hymes, L., & Hymes, J. (1964). *Oodles of noodles.* New York: Young Scott Books.

Kellogg, S. (1985). *Chicken Little.* New York: Mulberry Books.

Krauss, K. (1990). *I can fly.* New York: Golden Press.

Kuskin, K. (1990). *Roar and more.* New York: Harper Trophy.

Langstaff, J. (1955). *A frog went a courting.* San Diego, CA: Harcourt Brace.

Lansky, B. (1993). *The new adventures of mother goose.* Deerhaven, MN: Meadowbrook.

Lee, D. (1983). *Jelly belly.* Toronto, ON: Macmillan.

Leedy, L. (1989). *Pingo the plaid panda.* New York: Holiday House.

Lewis, K. (1999). *Chugga-chugga choo-choo.* New York: Hyperion.

Lewison, W. (1992). *Buzz said the bee.* New York: Scholastic.

Low, J. (1986). *Mice twice.* New York: Aladdin.

Martin, B., & Archambault, J. (1989). *Chicka chicka boom boom.* New York: Simon and Schuster.

Marzollo, J. (1989). *The teddy bear book.* New York: Dial.

Marzollo, J. (1990). *Pretend you're a cat.* New York: Dial.

O'Connor, J. (1986). *The teeny tiny woman.* New York: Random House.

Obligado, L. (1983). *Faint frogs feeling feverish and other terrifically tantalizing tongue twisters.* New York: Viking.

Ochs, C. P. (1991). *Moose on the loose.* Minneapolis, MN: Carolrhoda Books.

Patz, N. (1983). *Moses supposes his toeses are roses.* San Diego, CA: Harcourt Brace Jovanovich.

Pearson, M. (2000). *Pickles in my soup.* New York: Scholastic.

Perez-Mercado, (2000). M. M. *Splat!* New York: Scholastic.

Pomerantz, C. (1974). *The piggy in the puddle.* New York: Macmillan.

Pomerantz, C. (1987). *How many trucks can a tow truck tow?* New York: Random House.

Prelutsky, J. (1986). *Read-aloud rhymes for the very young.* New York: Knopf.

Provenson, A., & Provenson, M. (1977). *Old Mother Hubbard.* New York: Random House.

Purviance, S., & O'Shell, M. (1988). *Alphabet Annie announces an all-American album.* Boston: Houghton Mifflin.

Raffi. (1987). *Down by the bay.* New York: Crown.

Salisbury, K. (1997). *My nose is a rose.* Cleveland, OH: Learning Horizons.

Salisbury, K. (1997). *There's a bug in my mug.* Cleveland, OH: Learning Horizons.

Scarry, R. (1970). *Richard Scarry's best mother goose ever.* New York: Western.

Scarry, R. (2000). *The best storybook ever!* New York: Golden Books.

Schwartz, A. (1972). *Busy buzzing bumblebees and other tongue twisters.* New York: HarperCollins.

Sendak, M. (1962). *Chicken soup with rice.* New York: HarperCollins.

Sendak, M. (1988). *Where the wild things are.* New York: HarperCollins.

Serfozo, M. K. (1988).*Who said read?* New York: Macmillan.

Shaw, N. (1986). *Sheep in a jeep.* Boston: Houghton Mifflin.

Shaw, N. (1986). *Sheep on a ship.* Boston: Houghton Mifflin.

Showers, P. (1991). *The listening walk.* New York: Harper Trophy.

Silverstein, S. (1964). *A giraffe and a half.* New York: HarperCollins.

Slepian, J., & Seidler, A. (1988). *The hungry thing.* New York: Scholastic.

Wadsworth, O. A. (1985). *Over in the meadow.* New York: Penguin.

Winthrop, E. (1986). *Shoes.* New York: Harper Trophy.

Yektai, N. (1987). *Bears in pairs.* New York: Macmillan.

Zemach, M. (1976). *Hush, little baby.* New York: E. P. Dutton.

Alphabet Books

Blades, A. (1985). *By the sea: An alphabet book.* Toronto, Ontario: Kids Can Press.

Bond, M. (1996). *John Burmingham's ABC.* Dallas, TX: Crown.

Calmenson, S. (1993). *It begins with A.* Santa Clara, CA: Hyperion.

Demi. (1982). *The peek-a-boo book ABC.* New York: Random House.

Downie, J. (1988). *Alphabet puzzle.* New York: William Morrow.

Ehlert, L. (1989). *Eating the alphabet.* San Diego: Harcourt.

Folsom, M., & Folsom, M. (1986). *Easy as pie.* Boston: Houghton Mifflin.

Garten, J. (1964). *The alphabet tale.* New York: Random House.

Golding, K. (1998). *Alphababies.* New York: DK Publishing.

Grover, M. (1993). *The accidental zucchini.* San Diego: Harcourt.

Layne, S. L., & Layne, D. D. (2005). *T is for teachers: A school alphabet.* Chelsea, MI: Sleeping Bear Press.

Pienkowski, J. (1995). *A to Z sticker book.* New York: Random House.

Preller, J. (1997). *NBA action from A to Z.* New York: Scholastic.

Smith, M., & Smith, R. (2005). *Z is for zookeeper: A zoo alphabet.* Chelsea, MI: Sleeping Bear Press.

Snow, A. (1994). *The monster book of ABC sounds.* New York: Puffin.

Tucker, S. (1995). *A is for astronaut.* New York: Simon & Schuster.

Songs for Phonemic Awareness Development

Avni, F. — *Fiddle around with the middle sound*

Avni, F. — *Just one word*

Avni, F. — *Take a word apart*

Avni, F., & Schimmel, N. — *Syllable song*

Bethie. — *Really silly songs about animals*

Bollinger, C. — *Let's make a rhyme*

Brown, R. — *Echo game*

Brown, R. — *Let's rhyme with the animals*

Chorao, K. — *The baby's bedtime book*

Dines, K. — *Oodles and oddles of noodles*

Fixman, J. — *Phonogram funk*

Forster, J., & Chapin, T. — *I would if I could*

Gill, J. — *Drving here, driving there*
Gill, J. — *Tickle toe*
Guthrie, W. — *Songs to grow on*
Jenkins, E. — *You'll sing a song*
Lewis, M. — *Rhyme riddles*
MacDonald, S. — *I can't spell Ohio!*
Madsen, G. — *Old Mr. Mackle Hackle*
Palmer, H. — *Bounce!*
Palmer, H. — *Can a cherry pie wave goodbye*
Palmer, H. — *Chickadee and chipmunk*
Palmer, H. — *Classic nursery rhymes*
Raffi — *Willoughby wallaby woo*
Raffi — *Raffi's singable songbook*
Scruggs, — J. *Bahamas pajamas*
Seeger, M. — *American folk songs for children*
Whitfield, G. — *Apples and bananas*

Web Resources for Phonemic Awareness Development

ABC Teach: www.abcteach.com

Includes reading, writing, foreign language, and math activities for students, parents, and teachers. Features numerous free printable pages and worksheets and online tools for making a variety of documents such as puzzles, memory games, and printable booklets.

Carol Hurst's Children's Literature site: www.carolhurst.com

Features reviews of recommended books for children as well as suggestions for how to use them to enhance learning and integrate curriculum.

Early Childhood Education Network Literacy Center:
www.literacycenter.net

Provides literacy lessons for parents and teachers in four languages: English, Spanish, French, and German.

Early Childhood Network: www.literacycenter.net/lessonview_en.htm

Contains literacy lessons that highlight the alphabet, words, numbers, shapes, and colors.

Everything Preschool: www.everythingpreschool.com

Offers numerous early childhood education ideas separated into themes.

Early Reading Information: www.earlyreading.info
> Contains resources for kindergarten through third grade on phonemic awareness, phonics, fluency, vocabulary, and comprehension.

The Florida Center for Reading Research: www.fcrr.org
> Addresses a variety of reading-related topics for teachers, literacy coaches, administrators, parents, and researchers. For information on phonemic awareness, click first on "curriculum and instruction," then click on "K–1 student centered activities." There you'll find suggested strategies for building phonological awareness.

Preschool Express: www.preschoolexpress.com
> Contains preschool activities such as art, music, rhymes, and stories for each month.

Preschool Printables: www.preschoolprintables.com
> Includes reproducible, preschool-oriented games, lesson plans, and stories.

Preschool Rainbow: www.preschoolrainbow.org/book-themes.htm
> Features lists of classic and new educational picture books arranged by themes.

Reach Out and Read: http://reachoutandread.org
> Helps to cultivate early literacy skills by emphasizing the importance of reading aloud to young children as part of their pediatric care.

Reading Rainbow: http://pbskids.org/readingrainbow
> Features an online resource library, travel with LeVar Burton, contests, adventures, and interactive games.

Read Write Think (IRA/NCTE):
http://www.readwritethink.org/lessons/lesson_view.asp?id=120
> Contains lesson plans for grades K–12 with a second on "Reading Theory to Practice" for each lesson. Lessons are based on IRA and NCTE Standards.

Sesame Street: www.sesameworkshop.org/sesamestreet
> Contains a host of games and stories for young children based on the alphabet, art, and music. Suggestions for parents are also included.

Songs for Teaching: www.songsforteaching.com
> Features thousands of musical lyrics, sound-clips, and teaching suggestions for use across content areas. Research-based articles on how music promotes learning are also included.

Teacher Vision: www.teachervision.com
> Contains a lesson plan center, cross-curricular lessons, and graphic organizers. Membership required.

Word Play Website: www.wolinskyweb.net/word.htm
> Contains an alphabetized list of sites that promote play with words.

Professional Resources for Teachers

Adams, M. J., Foorman, B. R., Lundberg, I., & Beeler, T. (1998). *Phonemic awareness in young children: A classroom curriculum.* Baltimore, MD: Brookes.

Includes listening games and activities that focus on rhyming, alliteration, and segmentation. Assessment suggestions are included.

Blevins, W. (1999). *Phonemic awareness activities for early reading success.* New York: Scholastic.

Contains activities that teach phonemic awareness through poetry, rhymes, pictures, games, songs, and sounds.

Barone, D. M., & Morrow, L. M. (2002) *Literacy and young children: Researched-based practices.* New York: Guilford.

Offers research-based practices that teach young children to read and write. Includes fluency, home literacy, and teacher training practices.

Ericson, L., & Julieboaut, M. F. (1998). *The phonological awareness handbook for kindergarten and primary teachers.* Newark, DE: International Reading Association.

Features pre- and postassessments and activities for teaching young children through sound play and rhyming activities.

Fitzpatrick, J. (1997). *Phonemic awareness: Playing with sounds to strengthen beginning reading skills.* Cypress, CA: Creative Teaching Press.

Contains lessons to help children see the relationships between sounds. Rhyming, phoneme substitution, and phoneme blending activities are included.

Fitzpatrick, J., & Cernek, K. (Eds.). (2002). *Getting ready to read: Independent phonemic awareness centers for emergent readers.* Huntington Beach, CA: Creative Teaching Press.

Offers phonemic awareness strategies and activities for use in learning centers.

Fox, B. J. (2003). *Word recognition activities: Patterns and strategies for developing fluency.* Upper Saddle River, NJ: Pearson.

Includes hands-on activities for teaching word recognition and fluency.

Gunning, T. (2000). *Phonological awareness and primary phonics.* Boston: Allyn & Bacon.

Gives step-by-step instructional and assessment suggestions for phonological awareness and phonics.

Hajdusiewicz, B. B. (1998). *Phonics through poetry: Teaching phonemic awareness using poetry.* Upper Saddle River, NJ: Pearson.

Uses the rhythm and rhyme of 115 poems to teach phonics.

Lane, H. B., & Pullen, P. C. (2003). *Phonological awareness assessment and instruction: A sound beginning.* Boston: Allyn & Bacon.

Provides activities to assess phonological awareness for children in preschool through second grade.

McCormick, C. E., Throneburg, R. N., & Smitley, J. M. (2002). *A sound start: Phonemic awareness lessons for reading success.* New York: Guilford.
Contains lessons, suitable for whole group or individual instruction, for help-ing students develop phonemic awareness.

Neuman, S. B., & Roskos, K. A. (Eds.). (1998). *Children achieving: Best prac-tices in early literacy.* Newark, DE: International Reading Association.
Addresses the issue of providing effective instruction that meets the diverse needs of children ages 2 through 8.

Notari-Syverson, A., O'Connor, R. E., & Vaadasy, P. F. (1998) *Ladders to literacy: A preschool activity book.* Baltimore, MD: Brookes.
Provides activities for parents and teachers to use when helping emergent readers gain foundational literacy skills.

Opitz, M. (2000). *Rhymes and reasons: Literature & language play for phono-logical awareness.* Portsmouth, NH: Heinemann.
Offers an in-depth look at phonological awareness using rhyming texts, repeti-tive texts, and songs.

Rog, L. J. (2001). *Early literacy instruction in kindergarten.* Newark, DE: International Reading Association.
Includes developmentally appropriate activities to meet the diverse needs of kindergartners.

Roskos, K. A., Tabors, P. O., & Lenhart, L. A. (2004). *Oral language and early literacy in preschool: Talking, reading, and writing.* Newark, DE: In-ternational Reading Association.
Provides preschool teachers with strategies that promote talking, reading, and writing.

Strickland, D. S., & Schickendaz, J. A. (2004). *Learning about print in preschool: Working with letters, words, and beginning links with phonemic awareness.* Newark, DE: International Reading Association.
Provides teachers with effective strategies to help preschoolers learn concepts of print, phonemic awareness, and alphabet knowledge.

Wagstaff, J. M. (2001). *Irresistible sound matching sheets and lessons that build phonemic awareness.* New York: Scholastic.
Offers hands-on lessons using sound boards from 24 favorite stories to pro-mote phonemic awareness.

Yopp, H. K., & Yopp, R. H. (2003). *Oo-pples and boo-noo-noos: Song and activities for phonemic awareness.* Orlando, FL: Harcourt Brace.
Features tongue twisters, jump-rope rhymes, and other activities that enable children to explore different sounds. Includes a CD.

Zgonc, Y. (2000). *Sounds in action: Phonological awareness activities & assessment.* Woodstock, VT: Crystal Springs Books.

Provides phonological awareness activities and assessments to help children become successful readers. Includes a discussion of key research findings.

Goal Planning

As you reflect on your readings and discussions through your use of this professional development guide, consider your next steps for applying what you have learned to enhance your phonemic awareness instruction. Using the following chart, record the changes and refinements you would like to make to your current program. Then think about and record the materials and resources you will need in order to makes those changes. Finally, consider techniques you might use to evaluate the effectiveness of these changes.

Goal Planning: Phonemic
Awareness Assessment

Goal _____

Plans by _____ Date _____

Action Steps	Materials/ Resources	Evaluation

Summary: In light of all this, I will

Start doing

_____

_____

Stop doing

_____

_____

Do more of

_____

_____

Do less of

_____

_____

Book Club Ideas

*T*hroughout the book, you have seen icons indicating activities or discussion points that lend themselves to book club conversations. We hope you and your colleagues will take advantage of these opportunities. Our experience has taught us that learning from and with each other is a powerful way to promote innovation. In this appendix, we provide additional questions and ideas for discussion. They are organized according to the chapters in the book.

Introduction: Phonemic Awareness

- Look more closely at the report of the National Reading Panel. Make notes about key insights and the classroom implications of these insights. Share these with colleagues. (The report is available online at www.nationalreadingpanel.org. A shorter version is available at www.nifl.gov/partnershipforreading/publications/PFRbookletBW.pdf.)

- Select a piece of follow-up reading from the NRP website or at the National Institute for Literacy (http://nifl.gov). Make notes and share these with your colleagues.

- Think back to the beginning of your teaching career. What were you taught about teaching phonemic awareness? Share these insights with colleagues and together attempt to determine how the role of phonemic awareness in early literacy instruction has changed over time.

Chapter 1: Phonemic Awareness: What Does Research Tell Us?

- Make notes about the relationship between phonemic awareness and reading achievement. With your colleagues, write a paragraph that explains this relationship.

- Talk with colleagues about what may account for children's phonemic awareness difficulties. For each reason you can identify, make instructional plans for addressing it.

- Talk with colleagues about how you can draw attention to phonemic awareness during teacher read-alouds and students' guided reading lessons.

- Talk with colleagues about the implications of the phonemic awareness stages discussed in the chapter.

- Brainstorm with colleagues ways in which you can increase your emphasis on phonemic awareness instruction throughout the school day. Make concrete plans for integrating these ideas into your instructional routines.

Chapter 2: Instructional Strategies for Phonemic Awareness Development

- Decide on the two or three instructional activities best suited for your classroom. Explain to your colleagues why each activity is a good fit.

- For each activity selected, make plans for implementation. Keep track of questions. Share your plans with colleagues and discuss the questions.

- For each activity selected, make plans to assess impact. That is, how will you determine if these new activities are enhancing your students' phonemic awareness? Share your ideas with colleagues and invite them to offer feedback.

- If you are currently using a commercial phonemic awareness program, evaluate it using the questions posed at the end of the chapter. If your evaluation identifies weaknesses, discuss these with your colleagues. Make plans to strengthen these weak areas if possible.

Chapter 3: Assessing Phonemic Awareness Development

- Discuss each "big idea" about assessment in more detail. Decide if you agree or disagree with each, why, and what implications the ideas have for your classroom assessment plans for phonemic awareness.

- List all possible revisions to your classroom assessment plans for phonemic awareness. Then rank-order these. Explain your reasoning to your colleagues.

- For the most important revision idea from the activity above, develop an implementation plan. Share this with your colleagues and seek their feedback.

Chapter 4: Fostering Home–School Connections

- Develop detailed notes about the following: How do you currently explain phonemic awareness development to parents? What do you currently do to help parents see the role they play in promoting their children's phonemic awareness development?

- Review the chapter's suggested activities for supporting a child's phonemic awareness development at home. Select those activities that you believe would be useful and feasible for the families of your students. Make detailed plans for sharing the activities you selected with these families. For example, draft a newsletter that includes suggested phonemic awareness activities or plan an parent workshop in which you model home-based phonemic awareness activities.

- Outline your current parent-teacher conference format. Discuss the strengths and weaknesses of this format. Based on the suggestions offered in the chapter, and on your conversations with colleagues, consider revisions you could make to your conferences in order to increase their effectiveness.

Chapter 5: Resources

- Review the list of children's books recommended in the chapter for phonemic awareness development. Select two or more titles that you do not currently use with your students. Make plans for incorporating these sources in your instructional plans.

- The chapter provides lists of suggested alphabet books and songs for supporting phonemic awareness development. Discuss with colleagues other useful sources that you could add to these lists. Also discuss suggestions for ways in which these sources can be used with students.

- Search the Web for additional resources and sites that can provide support for phonemic awareness instruction.

Notes

*A*s you work through the book, you may want to make notes here about important ideas gleaned from discussions. You can keep track of additional resources. You may also want to use these pages to reflect on changes you made in your phonemic awareness instruction and to make notes about next steps.

General Issues and Ideas

Instructional Plans

Assessment Plans

Working with Home Partners

Notes

Resources for Teachers

References

Adams, M. (1990). *Beginning to read: Thinking and learning about print.* Cambridge, MA: MIT Press.

Adams, M., Foorman, B., Lundberg, I., & Beeler, T. (1998). *Phonemic awareness in young children: A classroom curriculum.* Baltimore, MD: Brookes.

Ball, E., & Blachman, B. (1991). Does phoneme awareness training in kindergarten make a difference in early word recognition and developmental spelling? *Reading Research Quarterly, 26,* 49–66.

Bradley, L., & Bryant, P. (1983). Categorizing sounds and learning to read: A casual connection. *Nature, 301,* 409–421.

Burgess, S. R. (1999). The influence of speech perception, oral language ability, the home literacy environment, and prereading knowledge on the growth of phonological sensitivity: A 1-year longitudinal study. *Reading Research Quarterly, 34,* 400–402.

Calfee, R. (1998). Phonics and phonemes: Learning to decode and spell in a literature-based program. In J. L. Metsala & L. C. Ehri (Eds.), *Word recognition in beginning literacy* (pp. 315–340). Mahwah, NJ: Lawrence Erlbaum.

Calfee, R. C., & Norman, K. A. (2000). Psychological perspectives on the early reading wars: The case of phonological awareness. *Teachers College Reading, 100*(2), 242–274.

Clay, M. (1985). *The early detection of reading difficulties.* Portsmouth, NH: Heinemann.

Cooper, J. D., & Kiger, N. D. (2005). *Literacy assessment: Helping teachers plan instruction.* Boston: Houghton Mifflin.

Cooter, R., Marrin, P., & Mills-House, E. (1999). Family and community involvement: The bedrock of reading success. *The Reading Teacher, 52,* 891–896.

Cunningham, A. (1990). Explicit versus implicit instruction in phonemic awareness. *Journal of Experimental Child Psychology, 50,* 429–444.

Cunningham, P. M. (2000). *Phonics they use: Words for reading and writing.* New York: Addison-Wesley.

Cunningham, P. M., Moore, S. A., Cunningham, J. W., & Moore, D. W. (2004). *Reading and writing in elementary classrooms: Research-based K–4 instruction.* Boston: Allyn & Bacon.

Darling-Hammond, L., & McLaughlin, M. W. (1995). Policies that support professional development in an era of reform. *Phi Delta Kappan, 76*(8), 597–604.

Day, J., Dommer, K., Mraz, M., & Padak, N. (2002). *OhioReads: Tutor training plus manual.* Columbus, OH: Ohio Department of Education.

Dugan, J. R., Brancato, B. A., & Smrekar, J. L. (2004). Tuning into the sounds of language: Teaching phonemic awareness through rhymes, songs, poetry, and children's literature. In J. R. Dugan, P. E. Linder, M. B. Sampson, B. Brancato, & L. Elish-Piper (Eds.), *Celebrating the power of literacy: 2004 College Reading Association Yearbook* (pp. 79–93). Commerce, TX: Texas A&M University-Commerce.

Ehri, L. C. (1979). Linguistic insight: Threshold of reading acquisition. In T. G. Waller & G. E. MacKinnon (Eds.), *Reading research: Advances in theory and practice.* (pp. 63–114). New York: Academic Press.

Ehri, L. C. (1984). How orthography alters spoken language competencies in children learning to read and spell. In J. Downing & R. Valtin (Eds.), *Language awareness and learning to read* (pp. 119–147). New York: Springer-Verlag.

Ehri, L. C., & Nunes, S. R. (2002). The role of phonemic awareness in learning to read. In A. E. Farstrup & S. J. Samuels (Eds.), *What research has to say about reading instruction* (pp. 110–139). Newark, DE: International Reading Association.

Elkonin, D. B. (1973). Reading in the USSR. In J. Downing (Ed.), *Comparative reading* (pp. 551–579). New York: Macmillan.

Ferguson, C. A. (1986). Discovering sound units and constructing sound systems: It's child's play. In J. S. Perkell & D. H. Klatt (Eds.), *Invariance and variability in speech processes* (pp. 36–51). Hillsdale, NJ: Lawrence Erlbaum.

Hall, D. P., & Cunningham, P. M. (1998). *Month by month reading and writing for kindergarten.* Greensboro, NC: Carson-Dellosa.

Hall, D., & Williams, P. (2001). *Predictable charts: Shared writing for kindergarten and first grade.* Greensboro, NC: Carson-Dellosa.

Harris, V. T. H., & Hodges, R. E. (1995). *The literacy dictionary: The vocabulary of reading and writing.* Newark, DE: International Reading Association.

Hatcher, P., Hulme, C., & Ellis, A. (1994). Ameliorating early reading failure by integrating the reaching of reading and phonological skills: The phonological linkage hypothesis. *Child Development, 65,* 41–57.

Hiebert, E. H. (1999). Text matters in learning to read (Distinguished Educator Series). *The Reading Teacher, 52,* 552–568.

International Reading Association. (1998). *Phonemic awareness and the teaching of reading: A position statement from the Board of Directors of the International Reading Association.* Newark, DE: Author.

Iversen, S., & Tunmer, W. (1993). Phonological processing skills and the Reading Recovery Program. *Journal of Educational Psychology, 85,* 112–126.

Juel, C. (1988). Learning to read and write: A longitudinal study of fifty-four children from first through fourth grade. *Journal of Educational Psychology, 80,* 437–447.

Jusczyk, P. W. (1995). Language acquisition: Speech sounds and the beginning of phonology. In J. L. Miller & P. D. Eimas (Eds.), *Speech, language, and communication* (pp. 263–301). San Diego, CA: Academic.

Liberman, I., Shankweiler, D., Fischer, F., & Carter, B. (1974). Explicit syllable and phoneme segmentation in the young child. *Journal of Experimental Child Psychology, 18,* 201–212.

Lindblom, B. (1992). Phonological units as adaptive emergents of lexical development. In C. A. Ferguson, L. Menn, & C. Stoel-Gammon (Eds.), *Phonological development: Models, research, implications* (pp. 131–163). Timonium, MD: York.

Lundberg, I., Frost, J., & Petersen, O. (1988). Effects of an extensive program for stimulating phonological awareness in preschool children. *Reading Research Quarterly, 23,* 263–284.

Mason, P. A., & Schumm, J. S. (2003). *Promising practices in urban reading instruction.* Upper Saddle River, NJ: Prentice-Hall.

McTighe, J., & Wiggins, G. (2004). *Understanding by design.* Alexandria, VA: Association for Supervision and Curriculum Development.

Metsala, J. L., & Walley, A. C. (1998). Spoken vocabulary growth and segmental restructuring of lexical representations: Precursors to phonemic awareness and early reading ability. In J. L. Metsala & L. C. Ehri (Eds.), *Word recognition in beginning literacy* (pp. 89–120). Mahwah, NJ: Lawrence Erlbaum.

Mraz, M., Dodd-Kinner, J., Gruhler, D., McKeon, C., Newton, E., Padak, N., & Peck, J. (2001). The principals' FAQ project: Research-based answers to parents' questions. *College Reading Association Yearbook.*

Mraz, M., Padak, N., & Baycich, D. (2002). *Literacy tips for children.* Ohio Literacy Resource Center. (http://literacy.kent.edu/Oasis/pubs/child_lit_tips.pdf)

National Reading Panel. (2000). *Report of the National Reading Panel: Teaching children to read, an evidence-based assessment of the scientific research literature on reading and its implications for reading instruction:*

Reports of the subgroups. Washington, DC: National Institute for Child Health and Human Development.

Opitz, M. (2000). *Rhymes and reasons: Literature & language play for phonological awareness.* Portsmouth, NH: Heinemann.

Phillips, L. M., Norris, S. P., & Mason, J. M. (1996). Longitudinal effects of early literacy concepts on reading achievement: A kindergarten intervention and five-year follow-up. *Journal of Literacy Research, 28,* 173–195.

Purcell-Gates, V. (2002). Family Literacy. In M. L. Kamil, P. B. Mosenthal, P. D. Pearson, & R. Barr (Eds.), *Handbook of reading research, volume III* (pp. 853–870). Mahwah, NJ: Lawrence Erlbaum.

Rasinski, T., & Padak, N. (2001). *From phonics to fluency: Effective teaching of decoding and reading fluency in the elementary school.* New York: Longman.

Rasinski, T., & Padak, N. (2004). *Effective reading strategies: Teaching children who find reading difficult* (3rd ed.). Upper Saddle River, NJ: Pearson.

Renyi, J. (1998). Building learning into the teaching job. *Educational Leadership, 55*(5), 70–74.

Senechal, M., LeFevre, J., & Thomas, E. (1998). Differential effects of home literacy experiences on the development of oral and written language. *Reading Research Quarterly, 33,* 96–116.

Shankweiler, D., & Liberman, I. Y. (1972). Misreading: A search for causes. In J. F. Kavanaugh & I. G. Mattingly (Eds.), *Language by eye and by ear* (pp. 293–317). Cambridge, MA: MIT Press.

Share, D., Jorm, A., Maclean, R., & Matthews, R. (1984). Sources of individual differences in reading acquisition. *Journal of Educational Psychology, 76,* 1309–1324.

Share, D., & Stanovich, K. E. (1995). Cognitive processes in early reading development: Accommodating individual differences into a model of acquisition. In J. S. Carolson (Ed.), *Issues in education: Contributions from psychology* (pp. 1–57). Greenwich, CT: JAI.

Stahl, S. A., & Murray, B. (1998). Issues involved in defining phonological awareness and its relation to early reading. In J. L. Metsala & L. C. Ehri (Eds.), *Word recognition in beginning literacy* (pp. 65–88). Mahwah, NJ: Lawrence Erlbaum.

Stanovich, K. E. (1994). Distinguished educator series: Romance and reality. *The Reading Teacher, 47*(4), 280–291.

Taylor, E., & Collins, V. (2003). *Literacy leadership for grades 5–12.* Alexandria, VA: Association for Supervision and Curriculum Development.

Tierney, R. (1998). Literacy assessment reform: Shifting beliefs, principled possibilities, and emerging practices. *The Reading Teacher, 51,* 374–390.

Torgesen, J. K., & Burgess, S. R. (1998). Consistency of reading-related phonological processes through early childhood: Evidence from longitudinal-correlational and instructional studies. In J. L. Metsala & L. C. Ehri (Eds.), *Word recognition in beginning literacy* (pp. 161–188). Mahwah NJ: Lawrence Erlbaum.

Treiman, R., & Baron, J. (1983). Phonemic-analysis training helps children benefit from spelling sound rules. *Memory and Cognition, 11,* 382–389.

Tunmer, W., Herriman, M., & Nesdale, A. (1988). Metalinguistic abilities and beginning reading. *Reading Research Quarterly, 23,* 134–158.

Vacca, J. L., Vacca, R. T., Gove, M. K., Burkey, L. C., Lenhart, L. A., & McKeon, C. A. (2006). *Reading and learning to read.* Boston: Pearson.

Wenglinsky, H. (2000). *How teaching matters: Bringing the classroom back into discussions of teacher quality.* Princeton, NJ: Educational Testing Service.

West, K. (1998). Noticing and responding to learners: Literacy evaluation and instruction in the primary grades. *The Reading Teacher, 51,* 550–559.

Yopp, H. K. (1992). Developing phonemic awareness in young children. *The Reading Teacher, 45,* 696–703.

Yopp, H. K. (1995). A test for assessing phonemic awareness in young children. *The Reading Teacher, 49*(1), 20–29.

Yopp, H. K., & Yopp, R. H. (2000). Supporting phonemic awareness development in the classroom. *The Reading Teacher, 54*(2), 130–143.

Children's Literature

Carle, E. (1975). *All about Arthur: An absolutely absurd ape.* London: Franklin Watts.

Crowley (1999). *Mrs. Wishy Washy.* Columbus, OH: Wright Group/McGraw.

Maass, R. (1992). *When autumn comes.* New York: Henry Holt & Co.

Rockwell, A. (1989). *Apples and pumpkins.* New York: Scholastic.